Dictionary of

ENGLISH WORD-ROOTS

ENGLISH-ROOTS
AND ROOTS-ENGLISH

BY BOB SMITH

Dictionary of
ENGLISH
WORD-ROOTS

ENGLISH - ROOTS

and

ROOTS - ENGLISH

with examples and exercises

Robert W. L. Smith

MISSION COLLEGE, SANTA CLARA, CA.

1982

LITTLEFIELD, ADAMS & CO.

Totowa, New Jersey

PRINTED IN THE UNITED STATES OF AMERICA

INTRODUCTION

There are no long words in the English language. Even the example listed in this dictionary under "coni"—which, at forty-five letters is the longest word in Webster's Unabridged—is only a succession of shorter pieces, each of which has a simple meaning of its own.

This book is about those fragments of words, which may be called bases or elements and prefixes and suffixes, or may all be lumped together under the frightening appellation "segmental morphemes." I have chosen to call them simply word-roots because they are indeed the roots from which the English language grows.

If you are already familiar with word-roots, you will not be surprised at the way English words—even technical words which look long and difficult—explain themselves to you on the pages which follow. You may be surprised, though, to see a greater variety of roots and examples than you have seen in one place before. And I'm sure you'll be happy to find that the reversal of the dictionary—the English-to-roots section—makes possible a number of exercises which could not otherwise be used.

But if you are new to the workings of word-roots, you're in for a surprise and a treat as you discover that even the most complex of words consists of very simple parts which are anxious to tell you all about themselves.

Just to prove it, why not start with a look at that "coni" word? It looks absolutely monstrous, but a few minutes of flipping these pages should tell you that the roots say: "lung-beyond-small-looking-silicon-volcanic-dust-condition."

Without looking it up in a regular dictionary, you'll probably decide as I have that this horrendous collection of letters refers to "a lung condition caused by ultramicroscopic volcanic silicon dust" and is probably a miners' disease.

Although the word-roots listed here derive from many sources, the book offers no dry-as-dust inquiry into ancient languages long since dead, but a simple waking to awareness of the realities of living English. You can start by flipping the pages of the dictionary sections to see how common and technical words jostle each other for position as members of the same word-root families: *dexterity* and *dextrocardia, parent* and *oviparous, Nevada* and *nivicolous*. But sooner or later you'll want to move to the back of the book and face the prospect of filling the blanks that are waiting there to teach you.

In both sections I have tried to present the material simply and to stay out of the way of your work—and fun. Nevertheless, I have aimed at total accuracy in every detail and have regularly checked the material against the many authorities listed in the bibliography. I could not have taken greater care if I had written the book for myself alone, because originally I did. It gives me great pleasure to share it now with you. May it serve you well.

R. W. L. S.

University of Santa Clara
Santa Clara, California

for the one
who is well-named
"God's gracious gift"

Table of Contents

PART ONE
DICTIONARY

SECTION 1

Roots-to-English

A

-a	*feminine* alumna Frederika Eugenia
-a	*Greek plural ending* phenomena criteria Lepidoptera
a-	*in, on, at* aboard aside asleep
-a	*Latin ending* formula lacuna scintilla
-a	*Latin plural ending* data agenda impedimenta
a-, an-	*not, without* atheist anarchy anonymous
ab-	*away, from* abnormal abduct abrasive
ab-	see **ad-**
-abad	*town, city* Hyderabad Ahmadabad Saidabad
abdomin	*abdomen* abdominal abdominoscopy abdominothoracic
-able	*able to (be)* portable curable tenable

-ac, -iac	*related to* maniac cardiac insomniac
ac. acr	*sharp* acute acrid acumen
ac-	see **ad-**
acanth	*thorn, spine* acanthology acanthopod acanthoid
acar	*mite* acariasis acaroid acaricide
-aceous	*having the quality of* herbaceous saponaceous cretaceous
acet	*vinegar* acetic acetate acetometer
acid	*sour, acid* acidity acidosis acidulous
acin	*grape* acinose aciniform acinotubular
-acious	*having the quality of* tenacious loquacious vivacious
-acity	*quality of* veracity tenacity loquacity
-acle	*that which* receptacle tentacle spectacle
acou, acu	*to hear* acoustic acouesthesia osteoacusis
acr	see **ac**
acro	*high, extremity* acrobat acrophobia acronym
act	see **ag**
actin	*ray* actinic actinide actinomyces
acu	see **acou**
-acy, -cy	*state, quality, act* infancy literacy accuracy

-ad	*group* triad myriad decade
✓ad-, ab-, ac-, af-, **ag-, al-, an-, ap-,** **as-, at-**	*to, toward, against* adhere advertise attend
adelph	*brother* Philadelphia adelphogamy adelphic
aden	*gland* adenoid adenitis adenectomy
adip	*fat* adipose adipocellular adiposuria
-ae	*Latin plural ending* alumnae nebulae antennae
aeg	*goat* aegis Aegopodium Aegocerus
aelur	see **ailur**
aene	*bronze, copper* aeneous aeneolithic aeneomicans
aer	*air* aerate aerodynamics anaerobic
aesthes	see **esthet**
aesthet	see **esthet**
aeth	*burnt, brown* aethogen Aethionema Ethiopia
af-	see **ad-**
aft	*behind* aft after abaft
ag-	see **ad-**
ag, ig, act	*to do, to drive* agent ambiguous counteract
agap	*love* Agape Agapanthus Agapornis
agaric	*fungus* agaric agariciform agaricoid

agath	*good* Agatha agathology Agathosma
-age	*state, quality, act* bondage courage portage
agla	*bright* aglaozonia Aglaspis Aglaonema
agog	*leader* pedagogue demagogue synagogue
agon	*struggle* agony protagonist antagonist
agor	*marketplace* agoraphobia allegory panegyric
agr	*field* agriculture agrarian agronomy
agra	*seizure* podagra agraphilydrus theragra
ailur, aelur	*cat* ailurophobia aelurophile Ailuropoda
-air	see **-aire**
-aire, -air	*one who, that which* corsair millionaire questionnaire
-al	*like, related to* maternal pedal tactual
al	*to nourish* alimentary alimony *alma mater*
al-	*the* alcohol algebra alfalfa
al-	see **ad-**
al	see **alter**
ala	*wing* alate alar alisphenoid
alam	*poplar* alameda Alamo Los Alamos
alb	*white* album albino albumen

alector, alectry   *cock*
                         alectoria   alectryomachy   alectryomancy

alectry   see **alector**

aleur   *flour*
                         aleurometer   aleuronoid   aleurone

alex   *to protect*
                         Alexander   alexin   alexocyte

alg   *pain*
                         neuralgia   nostalgia   analgesic

all   *other*
                         allergy   allegory   allomorph

allel   *mutually*
                         allelotropic   allelomorph   parallel

alt   *high*
                         altitude   altimeter   altar

alter, al   *other*
                         alternate   alien   altruist

alum   *bitter*
                         alum   aluminum   aluminium

alveol   *pit*
                         alveolar   alveolo-labial   alveus

am   *to love*
                         amiable   amorous   amateur

amar   *bitter*
                         amara   amarine   amaroid

amaur   *dark*
                         amaurosis   amaurotic   amaurornis

ambi-, amphi-   *both, around*
                         ambidextrous   amphibious   amphitheater

ambly   *dull*
                         amblyacousia   amblyopia
                         amblychromasia

ambul   *to walk*
                         ambulatory   amble   somnambulist

americ	*America* americium Americomania Amerind
amni	*bowl, amnion* amniogenesis amnion amniotic
amoeb	*change, amoeba* amoeba amoeboid amoebocyte
amphi-	see **ambi-**
ampull	*flask* ampulla ampulliform Ampullaria
amygdal	*almond, tonsil* amygdalectomy amygdaloid amygdalase
amyl	*starch* amylosynthesis amylase amyloclast
-an	*like, related to* urban agrarian American
-an, -ian	*one who* artisan magician optician
an	*ring, anus* anal anoscopy ano-coccygeal
an-	see **a-**
an-	see **ad-**
an-	see **ana-**
-ana	*information about* Americana Jeffersoniana Californiana
ana-	*up, back, again* anatomy analysis anchronism
anatol	*east* anatolian Anatole Anatola
-ance	*state, quality, act* dominance radiance resistance
-ancy	*state, quality, act* constancy buoyancy hesitancy
ancyl	see **ankyl**

-and	see **-end**
andr	*man* polyandry Andrew gynandromorph
-ane	*like, related to* urbane mundane humane
-aneity, -eity	*quality* simultaneity contemporaneity heterogeneity
anem	*wind* anemology anemometer anemography
-aneous	*having the quality of* instantaneous contemporaneous simultaneous
angel	*message, messenger, angel* angel evangelist angelica
angi	*vessel, blood vessel* angiograph angiectomy sporangiferous
angl	*English* Anglican Anglophobe Anglo-Saxon
angl	see **angul**
angui	*snake* anguiform anguiped Anguilla
angul, angl	*angle* triangle angulometer anguliferous
angust	*narrow* angustifoliate anguish Angostura
anima	*spirit* animal inanimate equanimity
ankyl, ancyl	*crooked* ankylosis ankylodactylia ancylostomiasis
ann, enn	*year* annual anniversary centennial
annel, annul	*ring* annular anneloid Annelida

annul	see **annel**
ans	*handle* ansate ansiform ansotomy
anser	*goose* anserine anseriform anserous
-ant	*one who, that which, -ing* participant pendant secant
ant-	see **anti-**
ante-	*before* anteroom antecedent antediluvian
anter-	*front, before* anterior anterodorsal anterospinal
anth	*flower* anther chrysanthemum anthology
anthrac	*coal, carbuncle* anthracite anthracoid anthrax
anthrop	*man, human being* anthropology philanthropist anthropomorphic
anti-, ant-	*against, opposite* antisocial antiseptic antithesis
antr	*cavern, sinus* antrum antroscope antrodynia
aort	*to lift, to hang* aorta aortic aortopathy
ap-	see **ad-**
ap-	see **apo-**
apert	*to open* aperture aperitif April
aph	see **hapt**
aphr	*foam* aphrolite aphrite Aphrodite
aphrodis	*Aphrodite (goddess)* aphrodisiac aphrodisia aphrodisiomania

api	*bee*
	apiary apian apiculture
apic	*top, extremity*
	apex apical apico-alveolar
apo-, ap-	*away, from*
	apogee apostle apheter
-apse	see **hapt**
apt, ept	*to adjust, to fit*
	aptitude adapt inept
aqua	*water*
	aquarium aquamarine aqueduct
aquil	*eagle*
	aquiline aquila eagle
-ar	*like, related to*
	circular ocular regular
-ar	*one who*
	liar beggar bursar
arachn	*spider*
	arachnid arachnoid arachnodactyly
arc	*bow, arc*
	arciform arcograph arcosolium
arch	*first, to rule*
	archenemy monarch anarchy
arct	*north, bear (animal)*
	Arctic Antarctic Arcteranthis
arct	*to press together*
	arctation coarctate aortarctia
-ard, -art	*one who (pejorative)*
	drunkard coward braggart
-ard	see **hard**
are	*space*
	area areola aerie
aren	*sand*
	arena arenicolous arenaceous

areo	*Mars (Ares)* areography areocentric Areopagus
argent	*silver* Argentina argentiferous argentaffin
argyr	*silver* hydrargyrum miargyrite argyrocephalous
arid	*dry, to burn* arid ardent arson
arithm	*number* arithmetic logarithm arithmomania
-arium	see **-ary**
arm	*arm, weapon* army armament alarm
arsen	*manly, arsenic* arsenious arsenotherapy Arsenoxenus
art	*art, skill, craft* artisan artifact artificial
-art	see **-ard**
art	see **arthr**
arter	*artery* arterial arteriosclerosis periarteritis
arthr, art	*joint* arthritis arthropod article
-ary	*like, related to* sedentary sanitary temporary
-ary	*one who* revolutionary reactionary lapidary
-ary, -arium	*place where* mortuary granary planetarium
as-	see **ad-**
asc	*bag* ascocarp ascospore ascidiform
ascid	see **asc**

-asia, -asis	*state, quality, act* euthanasia antonomasia metasomasis
asin	*jackass* asinine asininity easel
-asis	see **-asia**
-asm	*state, quality, act* sarcasm enthusiasm pleonasm
asper	*rough* asperity exasperate asperate
aspid	*shield* aspidate Aspidobranchia Aglaspis
-ast	*one who* enthusiast pederast scholiast
-aster	*inferior* poetaster criticaster oleaster
aster, astr	*star* asterisk astronaut disaster
asthm	*breathless* asthma asthmatic asthmogenic
astr	see **aster**
astragal	*ankle-bone* astragalus astragalectomy astragalotibial
at-	see **ad-**
-ate	*to make, to act* captivate dehydrate saturate
-ate	*one who, that which* advocate delegate aggregate
-ate	*having the quality of* literate affectionate passionate
athen	*Athena (goddess)* Athens athenaeum attic
ather	*gruel, fat* atheroma atherogenic atherosclerosis
athl	*contest, prize* athlete pentathlon decathlon

-atim	*in the manner of*
	verbatim seriatim guttatim
atlant	*Atlas (the Titan)*
	Atlantic Atlantis atlas
atm	*breath*
	atmosphere atmometer atmophile
atr	*black*
	atrocious atrocity atrabilious
atri	*atrium*
	atrial sino-atrial atriopore
audi	*to hear*
	audience auditorium inaudible
aug	*to increase*
	augment auction author
augur	*soothsayer*
	augur augury inauguration
aul	*flute, pipe*
	hydraulic aulophyte Aulostoma
aur	*air, breeze*
	aura aurophore soar
aur	*ear*
	auricular binaural auscultation
aur	*gold*
	auriferous aureole aureate
austral	*south*
	Australia australorbis australopithecus
auto-	*self*
	automobile autograph autonomous
aux	*increase*
	auxiliary auxocyte enterauxe
av	*to desire*
	avid avarice avaricious
avi	*bird*
	aviary aviator aviculture

ax, axon	*axis* axilla axofugal axonometer
axon	see **ax**

B

bacc	*berry* bacciferous bacciform baccivorous
bacch	*Bacchus (god)* bacchanal bacchanalian bacchic
bacill	*bacillus, small staff* bacilliform bacillophobia bacillemia
back	*back* backward aback bacon
bacter	*small staff* bacterium bactericidal bacteriophage
bak	*to bake* bakery batch Baxter
balaen	*whale* balaenoid Balaena Balaenoptera
balan	*acorn, gland, penis* balanophore balanitis Balanops
ball	*ball* balloon ballot bullet
ball	see **bol**
ban	*to proclaim, to banish* banns contraband bandit
bane	*death* bane baneful henbane
bank	*bench* bank bankrupt banquet
bapt	*to dip* baptize baptism pedobaptism

bar	*pressure, weight* barometer barograph isobar
bar-	*son of* Bartholomew *Bar Mitzvah* Bar-Jona
barbar	*stranger, foreign* barbarian barbarism Barbara
barr	*board, obstruction* barrier barricade barrister
bas, bat, bet	*to go, to walk* abasia acrobat diabetes
basi	*bottom* basilar basiplast basi-occipital
basil	*king, royal* basilica Basil basilisk
bass	*low* bass basset bassoon
bat	*to strike* combat batter debate
bat	see **bas**
bath	*deep* bathyscaphe bathysphere bathos
be-	*intensive, to make* bedeck bemuse bewhiskered
bead	see **bid**
beck	*sign* beck beckon beacon
bel	*bag, to swell* belly bellows Belgium
bell	*beautiful* belle belladonna embellish
bell	*war* belligerent bellicose rebellion
ben-	*son of* Benjamin Ben-Hur Ben-Gurion

bene-	*good, well* benefactor benevolent benediction
bengal	*Bengal (India)* Bengalese Bengali bungalow
ber	*to carry, to bear* bear birth bier
-berg	*mountain* iceberg Heidelberg Nuremberg
bert	*bright* Robert Albert Bertha
bet	see **bas**
bi-	*two* bicycle biped bigamy
bib	*to drink* imbibe bib bibulous
bibli	*book* bibliophile bibliography Bible
bid, bead	*to ask, to pray* bid forbid bead
bide	*to stay* bide abide abode
bil	*bile* bilious bilirubin biliverdin
bind	*to bind* bind band bond
bio	*life* biology autobiography antibiotic
blanc	*white, pale* blanch blank *carte blanche*
blast	*to sprout, bud* blastula blastogenesis odontoblast
blaw	*to blow, to swell* blow bladder blast
blaz	*torch* blaze blazer emblazon

bleach	*white, pale* bleach bleachers bleak
bled, blod	*blood* bleed bloody bless
blenn	*mucus* blennogenous blenniform balanoblennorrhea
blep	*to look, to see* ablepsia ablepsy hemiablepsia
blephar	*eyelid, cilium* blepharitis blepharoncus blepharoplast
bol, ball	*to throw* hyperbole metabolism embolism
bomb	*dull noise* bomb bombard boom
bon	*good* bonny *bon vivant* boon
bor	*farmer, peasant* neighbor boorish Boer
bord	*board* boarder border starboard
boreal	*north* boreal borealization *aurora borealis*
-borough	see **-bury**
bosc, bot	*to graze, plant* proboscis botany botanophile
botul	*sausage* botulism botuliferous botuliform
bou, bov	*cow, ox* bovine bucolic bugle
bov	see **bou**
bow	*to bend* bow elbow buxom
brac	*arm* bracelet embrace brace

brachi	*arm*
	brachiate brachial brachiopod
brachy-	*short*
	brachymorphic brachycephalic
	brachycardia
brad	*broad, wide*
	broad breadth Bradley
brady-	*slow*
	bradykinetic bradycardia bradylogia
bran	see **burn**
branchi	*gill, fin*
	branchia branchiopod Nudibranchia
brek	*to break*
	breaker broken brick
brest	*breast*
	abreast breastplate brisket
brev	*short*
	brevity abbreviate breviary
brew	*to ferment*
	brewery Brewster bread
-bridge, -bruck	*bridge*
	Cambridge Stourbridge Innsbruck
broc	*to stitch, to pierce, to tap (keg)*
	brocade broach broker
brom	*stench*
	bromine bromide podobromidrosis
bronch	*windpipe*
	bronchial bronchitis bronchoscope
bront	*thunder*
	brontosaur brontophobia brontometer
-bruck	see **-bridge**
brun	*brown*
	brunette bruin brunish
-brunn	see **-burn**

bry	*moss, to swell* bryology bryophyte embryo
bucc	*cheek, mouth* buccal buccolabial buccilingual
bul	*to will* abulia hyperbulia bulesis
bulg	*bag* bulge budget budgetary
bull	*bubble, seal* ebullient boil bulletin
-bund, -bond	*tending toward* moribund pudibund vagabond
-burg, -burgh	*fort, town* Hamburg Pittsburgh Edinburgh
burg	*shelter, town* burgess burglar burrow
-burgh	see **-burg**
burn, bran	*to burn* burn brand brandy
-burn, -brunn	*spring* Bannockburn Blackburn Schoenbrunn
burs	*bag, sack* bursitis disburse reimburse
-bury, -borough	*fort, town* Canterbury Salisbury Peterborough
butyr	*butter* butyric butyrin butyrometer
-by	*town* Derby Whitby Grimsby
byss, byth	*bottom, depth* abyss abysmal Bythites
byss	*linen, flax* byssus byssiferous byssinosis
byth	see **byss**

C

cac	*bad* cacophony cacogenics arthrocace
cad, cid, cas	*to fall, to happen* decadent coincidence casualty
cadm	*Kadmos (Greek hero)* cadmia cadmium calamine
caduc	*falling* caducibranch caducicorn ˙caducous
caec, cec	*blind* caecum cecitis caecostomy
caen	see **cen**
caes, ces	*blue* caesium cesium caesious
caesar	*(Julius) Caesar* caesarean czar Jersey
cal	*hot* calorie caldron calescent
calam	*reed* calamiferous Calamites Calamospermae
calc	*heel* recalcitrant calcaneus inculcate
calc	*lime* calcium calculate chalk
calce	*shoe* discalced calceiform Calceolaria
calcul	*pebble* calculate calculus calculiform
calli	*beautiful* calligraphy calisthenics calliope
calyc	*cup, bell* calyciflorous calyx chalice
calypt	*hidden, covered* calyptoblastic eucalyptus calypter

camer	*chamber* camera chamber comrade
camp	*field* campaign encampment champagne
campan	*bell* campanile campanology campaniform
campt	*curved* camptodrome Camptosorus camptosaur
campyl	*curved* campylodrome campylotropous campylognathia
can, cyn	*dog* canine canary cynic
can, con, ken	*to know (how)* can conning keen
can	*reed, tube, hollow* cannon canyon cane
can	*rod, rule* canon law canonical canonize
canal	*canal* canal canaliculus channel
cancel	*crossbar, lattice* cancellation chancellor chancery
cancer, chancr	*crab, cancer* cancer cancrology chancre
cand	*white, glowing* incandescent candid candle
cani	*gray* canities canitist caniceps
cant	*song* incantation canticle recant
cap	*cape* cap escape chapel
cap, cip, cept, ceive	*to take* capture intercept deceive

capill   *hair*
                    capillary   capilliform   Capillaria

capit   *head*
                    capital   decapitate   recapitulate

capn   *smoke*
                    capnomancy   hypercapnia   Capnodium

capr   *goat*
                    caper   capricorn   Capri

caps   *container, box*
                    capsule   encapsulate   casket

car   *dear*
                    caress   charitable   cherish

car   *vehicle*
                    car   chariot   carriage

carbo   *coal, charcoal*
                    carbon   carbohydrate   carbonuria

carcin   *crab, cancer*
                    carcinoma   carcinosis   carcinectomy

card   *heart*
                    cardiac   pericardium   endocarditis

cari   *decay*
                    caries   carious   carrion

carl   *man, freeman*
                    churlish   Carl   Charles

carn   *flesh, meat*
                    carnal   incarnate   carnivorous

carotid   *stupor*
                    carotid   carotic   caroticotympanic

carp   *fruit*
                    carpology   polycarpous   carpophagous

carp   *wrist*
                    carpus   carpal   metacarpal

carph   *straw*
                    carpholite   carphology   carphosiderite

cart
paper, card
card   chart   cartoon

cartilag
gristle
cartilage   cartilaginous   cartilaginoid

caryo-
see **karyo-**

cas
house
casino   Casablanca   cassock

case
cheese
caseate   casease   casein

cast
pure
caste   castigate   incest

-caster, -cester
camp, fort
Lancaster   Manchester   Winchester

cat
cat
tomcat   caterpillar   caterwaul

cat-
see **cata-**

cata-, cath-, cat-
down, away, thoroughly
catastrophe   catalogue   catholic

caten
chain
concatenate   concatenation   chain

cath, kath
pure
catharsis   cathartic   Katharine

cath-
see **cata-**

caud
tail
caudal   coward   cue

caul
stalk
cauliform   cauliflorous   caulotaxy

caust, caut
to burn
caustic   holocaust   cauterize

caut
see **caust**

cav
hollow
cave   concave   excavate

caval
horse
cavalry   cavalcade   chivalry

cec	see **caec**
cede, ceed, cess	*to go, to yield* recede proceed secession
ceed	see **cede**
ceive	see **cap**
cel	*heaven, sky* celestial Celeste ceiling
cel	see **-cele**
cel	see **coel**
-cele, cel	*tumor, hernia* gastrocele celectomy hydrocele
celer	*fast* celerity accelerate decelerate
cell	*to hide* cell cellar conceal
cell	*room, cell* cellular celliferous celliform
cen	*empty* cenotaph cenophobia cenanthous
cen, caen, -cene	*new, recent* cenogenesis caenopithecus Eocene
cen, coen	*common* cenobite coenesthesia coenoblast
-cene	see **cen**
cens	*to assess* censor censure census
cent	*hundred* century centipede centigrade
cente	*puncture* centesis cephalocentesis pneumonocentesis
centr	*center* concentric concentration centrifugal

cephal	*head* cephalic encephalitis brachycephalic
cept	see **cap**
cer	*wax* cerecloth ceroplastics ceromel
cerat	see **kerat**
ceraun, keraun	*lightning* ceraunograph ceraunophone keraunophobia
cerc	*tail* cercus homocercal cercopithecus
cere	*Ceres (goddess)* cereal cerium Ceres (asteroid)
cerebr	*cerebrum, brain* cerebral cerebration cerebrospinal
cern, cert	*to perceive, to make certain* discern ascertain certificate
cert	see **cern**
cerule	*blue* cerulean ceruleite cerulignol
cervic	*neck* cervix cervical cervicofacial
ces	see **caes**
cess	see **cede**
cest	*girdle* cestodiasis Cestoda Polycesta
-cester	see **-caster**
cet	*whale* cetology cetacean ceticide
chaet, chet	*bristle* chaetognath chaeta spirochete
chalaz	*hailstone, lump* chalazion chalaza chalazodermia

chalc   *copper, bronze*
         chalcocite   leucochalcite   chalcolithic

chamae   *low, earth*
         chameleon   chamaecephalic   chamomile

chancr   see **cancer**

charg   *to load*
         charge   discharge   cargo

charis   *favor, gratitude*
         eucharist   eucharistic   charisma

chasm   *opening*
         chasmogamy   chasmophyte
         chasmatoplasm

cheap   *to buy*
         cheap   cheapen   Chapman

cheil, chil   *lip*
         cheiloschisis   Chilopsis   Cheilostomata

cheir   see **chir**

chel   *hoof, claw*
         chelate   chelophore   chelicera

chem   *to pour*
         chemistry   alchemy   chemotropism

chen   *goose*
         chenopod   Cheniscus   Chenendroscyphia

chet   see **chaet**

chias   *chi-shaped (X)*
         chiasmus   chiastolite   chiastoneural

chil   see **cheil**

chil   see **col**

chili-   see **kilo-**

chio   see **chion**

chion, chio   *snow*
         chionanthus   chionablepsia   chiolite

chir, cheir   *hand*
         chiropractor   chiropodist   macrocheiria

chlor	*green*
	chlorine chlorophyll chlorosis
choan	*funnel*
	choana choanocyte choanosome
chol	*bile, gall*
	choleric melancholy cholera
chondr	*grain, cartilage*
	chondroma chondrectomy mitochondrion
chor	*area*
	chorepiscopus chorology chorography
chor	*to dance*
	chorus choreography chorea
chord	*string*
	chordate notochord Chordata
chori	*fetal membrane, skin*
	endochorion chorioretinal choroid
chorist	*separated*
	choristate choristoblastoma choristoma
chres	*use*
	catachresis chrestomathy chreotechnics
christ	*Christ, anointed*
	christen criss-cross cretin
chrom, chro	*color*
	chromosome achromatic panchromatic
chron	*time*
	chronic chronometer chronicle
chrys	*gold, yellow*
	chrysanthemum chrysalis chrysolite
chthon	*earth*
	autochthonous chthonophagia chthonian
chyl	*fluid, juice*
	chyliferous hypochylia chylocyst
chym	*fluid, juice*
	chymiferous chymogen parenchymous
cid	see **cad**

-cide, cis	*to kill, to cut* fratricide genocide incision
cili	*eyelash, eyelid* cilium ciliary supercilious
cimic	*bedbug* cimex cimicide cimicoid
cinct	*to bind* precinct succinct cincture
cinema-	see **kine-**
ciner	*ash* incinerator cinereous cinerarium
cion	*pillar, uvula* cionitis cionectomy cionocranial
cip	see **cap**
circul	*round* circular circulus circellus
circum-	*around* circumstance circumference circumnavigate
cirr, cirrh	*curl* cirrus cirriped cirrhitidae
cirr, cirrh	*yellow* cirrhosis cirrhotic cirrolite
cirrh	see **cirr**
cis-, citra-	*on this side* cisapline cis-Alleghany citramontane
cis	see **-cide**
cit	*to summon, to impel* citation incite excitement
citr	*citrus* citric citronella citron
citra-	see **cis-**
civ	*citizen* civil civilian civilization

clad   *sprout*
     cladophyll   acanthocladous   cladanthous

claim   see **clam**

clam   *bond, to stick*
     clam   clamber   climb

clam, claim   *to shout*
     clamor   proclamation   exclaim

clar   *clear*
     declare   clarify   clarity

clas   *to break*
     iconoclast   cranioclast   clinoclase

claud   *lame*
     claudication   Claude   Gladys

claus   see **clud**

clav   *club*
     claviform   clavicorn   Claviceps

clav   *key*
     conclave   clavicle   clavichord

clav   *nail*
     clavus   clavellated   clavelization

clavic   *clavicle*
     clavicula   clavicular   clavicotomy

-cle, -cule   *small*
     particle   corpuscle   molecule

clean   *clean*
     cleanse   cleanly   unclean

cleav   *to split*
     cleaver   cleavage   cleft

cleav   *to stick*
     cleave   cliff   clay

cleid, cleis   *key, clavicle*
     cleidocranial   cleidomancy   enterocleisis

cleis   see **cleid**

cler	*lot, portion* clergy cleric clerk
climac	*ladder* climacteric climax climacium
climat	see **clin**
clin, climat	*to lean, slope* recline clinic climate
cloac	*sewer* cloaca Cloacina Cloacitrema
clon	*spasm* clonus clonic clonicotonic
close	see **clud**
cloth	*cloth* clothing clothes clad
clud, clus, claus, close	*to close* include exclusive clause
clus	see **clud**
clype	*shield* clypeus clypeate clypeofrontal
cnem	*shinbone, tibia* cnemitis cnemoscoliosis platycnemic
cnid	*nettle* cnidoblast cnidocil cnidosis
co-	see **com-**
cobalt	*devil, cobalt* cobaltic cobaltiferous cobaltocyanic
cocc	*berry, spherical bacterium* coccigenic streptococcus staphylococcus
coccyg	*cuckoo* coccyx coccygeal coccygectomy
cochl	*shell, spoon* cochleate cochleariform cochlear
coct	*to cook* concoction decoct precocious

coel, cel	*hollow* coelenterate blastocoel hydrocoele
coeli	*belly* coeliotomy coelialgia coelioscopy
coen	see **cen**
cogn	*to know* recognize incognito connoisseur
cohort	*enclosure, garden* court cohort courtier
coin	see **cen**
col, chil	*cold* cold cool chilly
col	*to filter* percolate colander culvert
col	*large intestine* colon colic colonic
col, cult	*to till, to inhabit* colony cultivation culture
col-	see **com-**
cole	*sheath* coleus coleopteron coleorhiza
coll	*glue* collage colloid protocol
coll	*neck* collar decollete collopexia
color	*color* tricolor discolor coloratura
colp	*hollow, vagina* endocolpitis colposcope colpidium
colubr	*snake* colubrine Colubrina Coluber
columb	*dove, pigeon* columbine columbarium Columbiformes

com	*hair*
	comephorous comoid comet
com	*a revel*
	encomium comedy encomiastic
com	*to sleep*
	coma comatose cemetery
com-, co-, col-,	*with, together, intensive*
con-, cor-	compress contemporary cooperate
combur	*to burn up*
	comburimeter combustion
	comburivorous
come	*to come*
	income outcome welcome
comit	*companion*
	concomitant count (noble) constable
con	*cone*
	coniform conifer conical
con	see **can**
con-	see **com-**
conch	*shell*
	conch conchiform conchitic
cond	*to hide*
	abscond recondite Escondido
condyl	*knuckle*
	condyle condyloma condylura
coni, koni	*dust*
	pneumonoultramicroscopicsilicovol-
	canoconiosis
contra-, counter-	*against, opposite*
	contradict contrary counterspy
cop	*to cut*
	syncopate syncope apocopate
copi	*abundance*
	copious copy cornucopia

copr	*dung*
	coproma coprolith coprolalia
copul	*bond*
	copula copulative couple
cor	*doll, pupil (of eye)*
	isocoria coroplasty coreometer
cor	*leather*
	excoriate scourge cuirass
cor-	see **com-**
corac	*raven*
	coracidium coracite coracoid
corall	*coral*
	coralliform coralloid Corallorhiza
cord	*heart*
	cordial record concord
corn	*horn*
	unicorn cornucopia Capricorn
coron	*wreath, crown*
	coronation coronet coroner
corp	*body*
	corpse incorporate corpulent
cortic	*bark, rind*
	corticosterone corticifugal corticospinal
coryn	*club*
	Corynebacterium Corynomorpha
	Leucocoryne
cosm	*universe, harmony*
	cosmic cosmonaut microcosm
cosmet	*beauty, harmony*
	cosmetic cosmesis cosmetology
cost	*rib, side, coast*
	costal accost cutlet
cotyl	*cup*
	dicotylous cotyloid Cotylophora

counter-	see **contra-**
coup	*to cut, to strike* coupon coupe cope
course	see **cur**
cover	*to cover, to hide* covert discover curfew
cox	*hip* coxa coxosternal coxalgia
crac	see **crat**
crak	*to crack* crack crackle crash
crani	*skull* cranium pericranium intracranial
cras	*mixing* idiosyncrasy crasis Craseomys
-crat, crac	*to rule* democrat aristocracy Hippocrates
cre-	see **creat**
creat	*to make* creative creature recreation
creat, cre-, kre-	*meat, flesh* pancreas creosote kreotoxism
cred	*to believe* credible credit credential
crek	*to croak* creak croak cricket (insect)
crepit	*to crackle, to crack* crepitation decrepit decrepitude
cresc, crease, cret, cru	*to grow* crescendo increase accretion
cret	*chalk* cretaceous cretify cretification
cri	*to judge* criticize criterion crisis

cri	*a ram* criophore crioboly criosphinx
cric	*ring* cricothyroid cricoid cricotomy
crimin	*charge, crime* criminal incriminate recrimination
crin	*hair* criniculture crinigerous crinoline
crin	*lily* crinoid crinum Actinocrinus
crin	*to separate* endocrine crinogenic crisis
croc	*hook, bend* crochet crouch crotch
cruc	*cross* crucifix crusade cruise
crur	*shank, leg* crural crurotarsal Crurosaurus
crust	*hard covering* crust encrusted crustacean
cry, kry	*cold* cryogen cryotherapy kryokonite
crym	*frost, cold* crymotherapy crymodynia crymo-anesthesia
crypt, krypt	*hidden* crypt cryptic krypton
cryst	*crystal* crystallography phenocryst crystalliferous
cten	*comb* ctenoid ctenophore Ctenidae
cub	see **cumb**
-cule	see **-cle**

culp	*fault, blame* culprit culpable exculpate
cult	see **col**
cumb, cub	*to lie (down)* succumb incumbent incubator
cumber	*to obstruct* cumbersome encumber encumbrance
cumul	*heap* accumulate cumulative cumulus
-cund, -und	*like, related to* rubicund jocund rotund
cune	*wedge* cuneiform cuneate cuneonavicular
cup	*to desire* cupidity concupiscence Cupid
cupr	*copper* cuprite cupreous cupric
cur	*care* pedicure curator sinecure
cur, course	*to run* current concourse recur
curv	*curved* curvature curviform curvilinear
cuspid	*point* cuspid bicuspid cuspidate
cuss	*to strike* concussion percussion repercussion
custod	*guard* custody custodian custodial
cut	*skin* cuticle cutaneous subcutaneous
cutl	*knife* cutlass cutlery cutler
-cy	see **-acy**

cyan	*blue* cyanide cyanosis cyanoderma
cyath	*cup* cyathiform cyathozooid cyatholith
cycl	*circle* tricycle cyclone Cyclops
cym	see **kym**
cymb	*boat, bowl* cymbal cymbocephalic Cymbidium
cyn	see **can**
cypr	*Cyprus* Cypriot Cypro-Turkish copper
cyst	*bladder* cyst cystoscope nephrocystitis
cyt	*cell* cytology cytogenesis leucocyte

D

dacry	*tear (-drop)* dacrcyocyst dacryoma dacryocystitis
dactyl	*finger* dactylic pterodactyl date (fruit)
dal, tal	*valley* dale taler dollar
dam	*woman, lady* dame madam damsel
damn	*loss* damnation condemn indemnity
das	*dense* dasymeter dasyure Dasiphora
dat	see **don**
day	*day* daylight daisy dawn

de-	*away, down, negative* decapitate deciduous demerit
deal	*part* dealer ordeal dole
dear	*precious* dearth darling endearing
deb	*to owe* debt debit debenture
dec	*becoming (proper)* decent decorate indecorous
dec, deka	*ten* decimal December decimate
dei, div	*God* deity deify divine
dein	see **din**
deipn	*dinner* deipnosophist deipnophobia Deipnopsocus
deka	see **dec**
del	*to destroy* delete deletion indelible
delph	*dolphin* dephinium delphocurarine Delphinapterus
delt	*delta-shaped ($\triangle$)* delta deltaic deltoid
dem	*to judge* deem doom doomsday
dem	see **des**
demi-	*half* demigod demitasse demivolt
demo	*people* democracy epidemic demagogue
demon	*demon* pandemonium demonology demonolatry

dendr	*tree* dendrology philodendron rhododendron
dent	*tooth* dentist dentifrice dandelion
derm	*skin* dermatology epidermis hypodermic
des, dem	*bond, ligament* diadem arthrodesis desmopexy
desider	*to want* desideratum desire desirable
deuter	*second* deuterium deuterogenesis Deuteronomy
dextr	*right hand* ambidextrous dexterity dextrocardia
di-	*two* diphthong dioxide dichromatic
di-	see **dia-**
di-	see **dis-**
dia	*day* diary dial dismal
dia-, di-	*through, between* diameter diagonal dialogue
diabol	*devil* diabolical diabolism devil
dich-	*two* dichotomy dichoptic dichogamy
dict	*to speak* predict verdict malediction
dicty, dikty	*net* dictyogen dictyosome diktyonite
didym	*twin* didymolite neodymium gastrodidymus
dif-	see **dis-**

dig *to excavate*
dig   dike   ditch

digit *finger, toe*
digit   digital   digitalis

dign *worthy*
dignity   dignitary   condign

dikty see **dicty**

din, dein *terrible*
dinosaur   Dinotherium   Deinodon

din *whirling*
Dinobryon   Dinoflagellata   Melodinus

diplo- *double*
diploma   diplopia   diplococcus

dips *thirst*
dipsomania   dipsotherapy   Dipsosaurus

| **dis-, di-, dif-** *away, negative*
dismiss   differ   disallow

disc *disk*
discus   discomycete   dish

div see **dei**

doc *to teach*
doctor   doctrine   docile

dodeca- *twelve*
dodecahedron   dodecasyllable
dodecaphonic

dog, dox *opinion, praise*
dogma   orthodox   doxology

dol *grief*
doleful   condolence   Dolores

dolicho- *long*
dolichocephalic   dolichomorphic
dolichosaurus

dom *home*
domestic   domicile   majordomo

-dom	*state, quality* serfdom kingdom wisdom
domin	*master* dominate domineer dominion
don	*to do* done do deed
don, dat	*to give* donation condone data
dor	*gift* Theodore Dorothy Pandora
-dorf, -thorpe	*town* Düsseldorf Althorp Linthorpe
dorm	*to sleep* dormant dormitory dormouse
dors	*back (of body)* dorsal endorse dorsispinal
dos, dot	*to give* dose antidote anecdote
dox	see **dog**
dra	*to do* drama dramatic drastic
drag	*to draw* drag draw draft
drif	*to drive* drift adrift drive
drink	*to drink* drinker drunk drown
drip	*to drip* dripping drop dribble
drom	*to run, course* syndrome hippodrome hemodrometer
dryg	*dry* dry drug drought
du-	*two* dua! duplex duplicate

duc	*to lead* produce abduct duchess
dulc	*sweet* dulcet dulcimer douceur
duodec-, **duoden-**	*twelve* duodecimal duodenary duodenum
duoden-	see **duodec-**
dur	*hard, lasting* durable obdurate enduring
dy-	*two* dyarchy dyad dyotheism
dyn, dynam	*power* dynamite dynasty thermodynamics
dynam	see **dyn**
dys-	*bad, badly* dystrophy dysentery dysplastic
dysi	*clothing* ecdysis ecdysiast endysis

E

e-, ex-	*out, away* emit expulsion exhale
eburn	*ivory* eburnean eburnation eburnated
ec-	*out, away* eccentric ecstasy ectopic
eccles	*church* ecclesiastical ecclesiarch ecclesiology
ech	*sound* echo catechumen catechism
ech	see **hec**
echin	*spiny* echinoderm echinosis Echinomastus

eco-, oec	*home* economy ecumenical androecium
ecto-	*outer, outside* ectoderm ectomorphic ectoplasm
edaph	*bottom, ground* edaphic edaphology edaphosauria
edema	*to swell* edema edematous edematigenous
-ee	*one who (passive)* divorcee employee payee
-eer	*one who* volunteer mutineer auctioneer
ef-	see **e-**
ego	*I, self* egotist egocentric *alter ego*
eid	see **id**
eido	*resemblance, form* eidoptometry Eidotheca Eidothrips
-eity	see **-aneity**
-ek, -ik	*descendant of, little* Adamek Gromek Lukasik
-el	*little, small* parcel novel cerebellum
elaph	*deer* elaphomyces elaphodus elaphoglossum
elaphr	*light (in weight)* Elaphrium Elaphrocnemus Elaphrus
elasm	*metal plate* elasmobranch elasmothere elasmosaur
electr	*electric, amber* electricity electrode electrolysis
eleuther	*free* eleutheromania eleutheropetalous Eleutherodactylus

-em	*something done* system theorem stratagem
em-	see **en-**
em	see **hem**
-eme	*something done* grapheme morpheme phoneme
emet	*to vomit* emetic emesis emetatrophia
empt	*to buy, to take* exempt redemption example
en-, em-	*in, into, intensive* enclose parenthesis enliven
-en	*to make* weaken harden loosen
-en	*having the quality of* wooden rotten woolen
-ence	*state, quality, act* dependence residence competence
encephal	*brain* encephalitis encephalography metencephalon
-ency	*state, quality, act* consistency despondency urgency
-end, -and	*to be done* agenda addenda memorandum
-end, -and	*-ing* friend fiend errand
endo-	*inside* endoderm endocranium endocrine
engy-	*near* engyseismology Engystoma Engyptilla
enigm	*puzzle* enigma enigmatic enigmatography
enn	see **ann**

ennea-	*nine*
	ennead enneagon enneapetalous
ens	*sword*
	ensiform Ensis ensisternum
-ent	*like, related to, -ing*
	benevolent consequent nascent
-ent	*one who, that which, -ing*
	president tangent regent
ent	see **ess**
enter-, entre-	*between*
	enterprise entertain entrepreneur
enter	*intestine*
	dysentery enterogastritis enterology
ento-	*within*
	entozoic entoderm entamoeba
entom	*insect*
	entomology entomotomy entomophagous
entre-	see **enter-**
eo-	*early, dawn*
	eolithic eosin Eoanthropus
-eous	*like, having the quality of*
	igneous aqueous vitreous
ep	*word, tale*
	epic epos orthoëpy
ep-	see **epi-**
epi-, ep-	*on, outside*
	epidemic epidermis epitaph
ept	see **apt**
equ	*equal*
	equation Equator equivocate
equ	*horse*
	equine equestrian equitation
-er	*more*
	wiser harder weaker

-er, -yer	*one who, that which* worker lawyer washer
ere	*sooner, before* ere erstwhile early
erem	*alone* eremite eremitic hermit
erg, urg	*work, power* energy ergophobia metallurgy
-erly	*direction whence* northerly southerly westerly
-ern	*related to* eastern western leathern
ero	*to love* erotic erogenous erotomania
-ero	*one who, that which* torero sombrero vaquero
err	*to wander* error erratic aberration
-ery	*place where* bakery brewery bindery
-ery, -ry	*state, quality, act* slavery drudgery bigotry
erythr	*red* erythroblast erythrocyte erythroderma
-escent	*becoming* adolescent obsolescent convalescent
eschat	*last* eschatology eschatological eschatin
-ese	*like, related to* Burmese Maltese pekingese
-esis	*state, quality, act* genesis exegesis poiesis
eso-	*within* esoteric esoneural esotropia
eso	see **oiso**

-esque	*in the manner of* picturesque statuesque Romanesque
ess, ent	*to be* essential interest entity
-ess	*feminine* goddess actress mistress
-est	*most* softest fastest loudest
esthet, esthes	*feeling* esthetic anesthetic kinesthetic
-et	see **-ette**
eth	*character, custom* ethical ethics ethos
ether	*upper air, to burn* ethereal ethyl ester
ethm	*sieve, perforated* ethmoid ethmolith ethmosphenoid
ethn	*race, nation* ethnic ethnology ethnolinguistics
etio-	*cause* etiology etiogenic etiopathology
-ette, -et	*little, small* cigarette closet cabinet
-ety	*state, quality, act* satiety society propriety
etym	*true* etymology etymologist etymography
eu-	*good, well* euphony eulogy Eugene
-eur	*one who* amateur entrepreneur connoisseur
euro-	*east* Euraquilo Euroclydon Euros
eurot	*mold* eurodontia eurotophila Eurotia

*eury-	*wide*
	eurycephalic euryplastic eurytopic
euthy-	*straight*
	euthyneura euthyphoria euthoscopic
ev	*age, time*
	medieval longevity primeval
ex-	see **e-**
exo-	*outside*
	exopathic exotic exotoxin
exter-	*outside*
	exterior external extrinsic
extra-	*outward, outside*
	extraordinary extracurricular extralegal
-ez	*descendant of, son of*
	Jimenez Perez Rodriguez

F

fa, fess	*to speak*
	fable nefarious profess
fac, fic, fect, -fy	*to do, to make*
	factory beneficial magnify
fac	*face*
	deface surface facade
falc	*curved, sickle*
	falciform falcate falcular
fall, fals	*to deceive*
	infallible fallacy falsify
fals	see **fall**
far	*flour, grain*
	farina farinaceous farrago
farc	*to stuff*
	farce infarct farctate

fare	*to go* farewell thoroughfare welfare
fasci	*band* fascia fascicle fasciorrhaphy
fatu	*foolish* fatuous fatuity infatuation
fav	*honeycomb* favella faveolate faviform
fe	*cattle, money, property* feudalism fee fellow
febr	*fever* febrile febrifuge febricity
fect	see **fac**
fed	*to feed* fed food foster
fel	*cat* feline feliform felicide
felic	*happy* felicity felicitation infelicitous
femin	*woman* feminine effeminate female
femor	*thigh* femoral femorotibial femorocele
fend	*to strike* fender defend fence
fenestra	*window* fenestral fenestrated defenestration
fer	*to carry* transfer fertile conference
-ferous	*bearing, causing* mortiferous coniferous vociferous
ferr	*iron* ferrous ferroprotein ferriferous
ferv	*to boil, to bubble* fervor fervent effervescent

fess	see **fa**
fest	*feast* festive festival festoon
fet	*to stink* fetid fetor asafetida
fet	*unborn child* fetal fetoplacental effete
fet	see **fot**
fibr	*fiber* fibroblast fibrin chondrofibroma
fibul	*pin, buckle* fibula fibulocalcaneal Fibularia
fic	see **fac**
fid	*faith* fidelity confident infidel
-fid	see **fiss**
fig	*to fashion* figure figment effigy
fil	*son* filial affiliate FitzGerald
fil	*thread* filament file profile
fimbr	*fringe* fimbriated fimbriodentate Fimbristylus
fin	*end, limit* final infinite definition
firm	*strong* confirm infirmary affirm
fiss, -fid	*to split* fission fissure bifid
fitz-	*son of* FitzGerald Fitzpatrick Fitzsimmons
fix	*to fasten* prefix suffix transfix

| **fla** | *to blow* |
| | inflate   deflate   flavor |

| **flabell** | *breeze* |
| | flabellum   flabellifoliate   flute |

| **flagell** | *whip* |
| | flagellant   flagellation   flail |

| **flagr** | *to burn* |
| | flagrant   conflagration   effulgent |

| **flam** | *flame* |
| | flammable   inflammatory   flamboyant |

| **flam** | see **flem** |

| **flav** | *yellow* |
| | riboflavin   flavid   flavescence |

| **flect, flex** | *to bend* |
| | deflect   reflection   circumflex |

| **fledge** | *feathered, mature* |
| | unfledged   full-fledged   fledgeling |

| **flem, flam** | *Flemish* |
| | Flemish   flamenco   flamingo |

| **flex** | see **flect** |

| **flict** | *to strike* |
| | inflict   afflict   conflict |

| **flor** | *flower* |
| | floral   florist   Florida |

| **flot** | *to float* |
| | float   flotilla   flotsam |

| **flu, flux** | *to flow* |
| | fluid   superfluous   influx |

| **flux** | see **flu** |

| **foc** | *focus* |
| | focal   bifocals   focimeter |

| **-fold** | *-fold, times* |
| | tenfold   hundredfold   manifold |

| **foli** | *leaf* |
| | foliage   exfoliate   portfolio |

folk	*people* folk folklore Volkswagen
foll	*bellows, windbag, bag* follicle folly fool
for-	*against, away* forbid forsake forswear
for	*door, opening, outdoors* perforation forum forest
foramin	*opening* foraminal foraminulum Foraminites
-ford	*(river) ford* Oxford Stafford Bradford
fore-	*before* foresee forewarn forecast
form	*form, shape* uniform conformity reformation
formic	*ant* formic formicivorous Formica
fornic	*arch* fornix fornicate fornicolumn
fort	*strong* fortify fortitude comfort
foss	*ditch* fossa fossulate fossorial
fot, fet	*foot* foot feet fetter
found	see **fund**
found	see **fus**
fract	see **frag**
frag, fract	*to break* fragment fraction fracture
franc	*free, French* franchise Francis Franco-American
frater	*brother* fraternal fraternize confraternity

fre	*to love* free freedom friend
fric	*to rub* friction dentifrice fricative
frig	*cold* frigid frigescent refrigerator
front	*forehead* front confront frontier
fruct	*full enjoyment* fructify fruition fruit
fug	*to flee* fugitive refugee centrifugal
ful	*filthy* foul filth befoul
-ful	*having the quality of* cheerful hopeful remorseful
fulv	*orange* fulvous fulvescent fulvene
fum	*smoke* fume fumigate perfume
fun	*rope* funicular funambulist funiculus
funct	*to perform* function perfunctory defunct
fund, found	*to base, to establish* fundamental foundation profound
fund	see **fus**
furc	*fork* bifurcated furciform furciferous
fus, fund, found	*to pour* transfusion refund foundry
fusc	*dark, tawny* fuscous fuscochlorin fuscoferruginous
-fy	see **fac**

G

gal	*to sing, to scream* gale nightingale yell
galact	*milk* galaxy galactic dysgalactia
gall	*French* Gallic gallium Gallophobe
gam	*marriage* bigamy polygamy monogamous
gangli	*knot* ganglion gangliectomy gangliocyte
gar	*to protect, to supply* garrison garment garnish
gast	*to terrify* ghastly aghast ghost
gastr	*stomach* gastric gastritis gastronomy
ge	*earth* geometry geology apogee
geard	*enclosure, garden* garden yard orchard
gel	*frost* gelid gelatin congeal
gel, gelot	*to laugh* gelotherapy gelotometer gelogenic
gelot	see **gel**
gemin	*twin* gemini quadrigeminal gemination
gemm	*bud* gem gemmiform gemmologist
gen	*cause, birth, kind, race* generate homogenized genocide
gen, gon	*knee* genuflection goneitis gonyocele

georg	*farmer* George georgic Georgia
ger	*old* geriatrics gerontology gerontocracy
ger	*spear* Gerald Roger Gerard
ger	see **gest**
geran	*crane (bird)* geranium pedigree crane
germ	*bud* germinal germinate ovigerm
german	*German* Germanic germanium germanite
gest, ger	*to bear, to carry* belligerent congestion gesture
get	*to get* forget beget gotten
gif	*to give* gift given forgive
gigant	*giant* gigantic giganticide gigantomachy
gingiv	*gums* gingivitis gingival gingivolabial
glac	*ice* glacial glacier glaciology
gladi	*sword* gladiolus gladiator gladiatorial
glauc	*gray-green* glaucoma glaucous glauconite
gli	*glue* glioma gliacyte neuroglia
glob	*sphere* globe globule hemoglobin
glochi	*projecting* glochidium glochidial Triglochin

glom	*ball of yarn* glomus glomerulus conglomeration
gloss, glot	*language, tongue* glossary polyglot epiglottis
glot	see **gloss**
gluc	see **glyc**
glute	*rump, buttocks* gluteus gluteal gluteofemoral
glutin	*glue* gluten glutinous agglutination
glyc, gluc	*sweet* glycerine hypoglycemia glucose
glyph	*to carve* hieroglyphics solenoglyph glyph
gnath	*jaw* prognathous gnathitis gnathoplasty
gnom	see **gnos**
gnos, gnom	*to know* prognosis agnostic gnome
god	*God* goddess godsend gossip
gon	*angle, corner* pentagon trigonometry orthogonal
gono-	*reproductive* gonophore gonocyte gonococcus
gorg	*throat* gorge disgorge regurgitate
-gorod	see **-grad**
gos	*goose* gosling gossamer goosneck
-grad, -gorod	*city* Petrograd Leningrad Novgorod
grad, gress	*to step* gradual graduate regression

gram	see **graph**
gramin	*grass* gramineous graminivorous graminoid
gran	*grain* granary granite lipogranuloma
granat	*grainy* pomegranate grenade garnet
grand	*great* grand aggrandisement grandeur
graph, gram	*to write* biography graphite telegram
grat	*free, thankful, pleased* gratuity gratitude congratulate
grav	*to dig* grave engrave groove
grav	*to weigh, heavy* gravity gravitate aggravate
greg	*flock* congregation segregate gregarious
gregor	*watchman* Gregory Gregorian Grigorevich
gress	see **grad**
grip	*to seize* grip gripe grope
gross	*large* gross grocer engross
grow	*to grow* growth green grass
grund	*bottom* ground groundwork groin
guad	*river* Guadalupe Guadalajara Guadarama
guan	*dung* guano guaniferous guanophore

guerr	*war* guerrilla *nom de guerre c'est la guerre*
gust	*taste* gusto gustatory disgust
gutt	*drop* guttatim gutter gout
guttur	*throat* guttural gutturophony gutturonasal
gym	*naked, nude* gymnasium gymnospore gymnoblast
gyn	*woman* gynecology misogynist gynophobia
gyr	*ring, circle* gyration gyroscope gyrospasm

H

hab	*to have* habit exhibit ability
haem-	see **hem**
hagi	*holy* hagiography hagiarchy hagiolatry
hal	*a salt* halide halogen halophile
hal	*whole, healthy, holy* hale health halibut
hald	*to hold* halt held behold
ham, -heim, home	*home, town* Nottingham Mannheim homestead
hang	*to hang* hanger hanker hinge
haph	see **hapt**

| **haplo-** | *single* |
| | haploid   haplodont   Haplotaxidae |

| **hapt, haph, aph, apse** | *to touch* |
| | haptephobia   haphalgesia   synapse |

| **hard, -ard** | *hard* |
| | hardship   billiards   Leonard |

| **hatch** | *to chop* |
| | hatchet   crosshatch   hash |

| **haut** | *high* |
| | hauteur   *haute couture*   Terre Haute |

| **hav** | *to have* |
| | have   misbehave   behaviorism |

| **hears** | *harrow, to harrow* |
| | hearse   rehearse   rehearsal |

| **heart** | *heart* |
| | hearty   heartless   dishearten |

| **heath** | *wasteland* |
| | heathen   heather   hoyden |

| **hebdomad** | *week* |
| | hebdomad   hebdomadal   hebdomadary |

| **hebe** | *young* |
| | hebephrenia   hebeanthous   hebetic |

| **hebet** | *dull* |
| | hebetude   hebetate   hebetation |

| **hec, hex, ech** | *to hold* |
| | hectic   cachexy   epoch |

| **hecto-, hecato-** | *hundred* |
| | hectometer   hectograph   hecatomb |

| **hedon** | *pleasure* |
| | hedonism   hedonistic   hedonophobia |

| **hedr** | *seat, side* |
| | cathedral   polyhedron   sanhedrin |

| **heim** | see **-ham** |

| **hel** | *to hide* |
| | helmet   hell   hall |

heli	*sun*	
	heliotrope helium heliocentric	
helic	*spiral*	
	helicopter helical helix	
helminth	*worm*	
	helminthiasis platyhelminth Sterelmintha	
hem, haem, em	*blood*	
	hematology hemorrhage toxemia	
hemer	*day*	
	ephemeral hemerology hemerobious	
hemi-	*half*	
	hemisphere hemiplegic hemistich	
hen	*one*	
	hyphen henogenesis enosis	
hepat	*liver*	
	hepatic hepatitis gastrohepatic	
hept-	*seven*	
	heptameter heptatomic heptavalent	
her	*to hear*	
	hearing hearsay harken	
her, hered	*heir*	
	inherit heritage heredity	
her, hes	*to stick*	
	inherent coherence adhesive	
herb	*grass*	
	herbal herbarium herbivorous	
hered	see **her**	
herm	*Hermes*	
	hermetic hermetically hermaphrodite	
herpet	*snake*	
	herpes herpetology herpetic	
hes	see **her**	
hesper	*west, evening*	
	Hesperian hesperanopia vespers	

hetero-	*other*
	heterogeneous heterodox heterodyne
heur	*to find*
	heuristic heuretic Eureka
hev	*to lift*
	heave heavy upheaval
hexa-	*six*
	hexagon hexahedron hexachlorophene
hiat	*gap*
	hiatus hiatopexia hiation
hibern	*Irish*
	Hibernian Hibernophile Hibernology
hibern	*winter*
	hibernate hibernaculum hibernoma
hidr	*sweat*
	hyperhidrosis hidradenitis hidrocystoma
hier	*sacred*
	hierarchy hieroglyphics hierocracy
hilar	*merry*
	hilarious exhilarate Hilary
hipp	*horse*
	hippopotamus hippodrome Hippocrates
hispan, span	*Spanish*
	Hispanic Hispanophobe spaniel
hist	*tissue*
	histology histogenesis histolysis
hol	*hole*
	hole hollow hold (ship)
hol	*whole*
	holocaust holograph catholic
hol	*whole, healthy*
	holy holiday hollyhock
homo	*man, human being*
	homo sapiens homicide homage

homo- *same*
homogeneous   homosexual   homonym

-hood *state, quality*
manhood   childhood   knighthood

hor *to bound, to define*
horizon   aphorism   aorist

hor *hour*
horoscope   horology   horography

hormon *to excite*
hormone   hormonology   hormonoprivia

horr *to bristle*
horror   horrible   abhorrent

hum *ground*
humus   exhume   humiliate

hum *liquid*
humor   humidity   humidor

hunt *to pursue, to seize*
hunter   hint   hit

hus, hous *house*
housewife   husband   husk

hyal *glass*
hyalescence   hyalite   hyaloid

hydat *water*
hydatid   hydatism   hydatogenesis

hydr *water*
hydrant   dehydrate   hydrogen

hyet *rain*
hyetometer   hyetology   hytography

hygi *health*
hygiene   hygienic   hygeiolatry

hygr *wet*
hygrometer   hygrology   hygrothermal

hyl, yl *wood, matter, substance*
hylomorphism   hylozoism   cacodyl

hymen   *membrane*
                     hymen   hymenicolar   hymenopterous

hyo-   *upsilon-shaped (U)*
                     hyoid   hyothyroid   hyoglossus

hyp-   see **hypo-**

hyper-   *over, above*
                     hyperactive   hypersensitive   hypertension

hyperbor   *north*
                     hyperborean   hyperboreal   Hyperborea

hypn   *sleep*
                     hypnotic   hypnosis   hypnophobia

hypo-, hyp-   *under*
                     hypodermic   hypofunction   hypotenuse

hyps   *high*
                     hypsography   hypsicephalic   hypsodont

hyster   *womb*
                     hysteria   hysterectomy   colpohysteropexy

I

-i   *Latin plural ending*
                     alumni   cacti   radii

-ia   *condition*
                     anemia   pneumonia   tachycardia

-ia   *flower (name)*
                     begonia   fuchsia   dahlia

-iac   see **-ac**

-ian   see **-an**

-iasis   *condition*
                     scoleciasis   elephantiasis   taeniasis

iatr   *healing*
                     psychiatrist   pediatrician   geriatrics

ibi   *there*
                     alibi   ibid.   ibidem

-ible	*able to be* audible visible intangible
-ic	*like, related to* heroic optic rustic
-ical	*like, related to* spherical theatrical juridical
-ice	*act of, time of* service justice novice
ichthy	*fish* ichthyology ichthyosis ichthyoid
icon	*image* iconoclast iconolatry iconostasis
-ics	*science, system* physics ethics linguistics
-id	*like, related to* vivid fluid lucid
id, eid	*to see* idea ideal eidetic
-ida	*group* Arachnida Annelida Tricladida
ident	*same* identity identification identical
ideo-	*idea* ideology ideogram ideogeny
idio-	*personal* idiom idiosyncrasy idiopathic
idol	*image* idolatry idolize idoloclast
-ie	see **-y**
-ier	*one who* cashier courier financier
ig	see **ag**
ign	*fire* ignite ignition igneous

-ik	see **-ek**
il-	see **in-**
-ile	*able to (be)* fertile mobile docile
ile	*ileum, groin* ileostomy ileitis ileocolostomy
-ile	*like, related to* puerile tactile juvenile
ili	*ilium, groin* iliac iliosacral iliofemoral
| **im-**	see **in-**
in	*fiber* inosteatoma initis inogen
| **in-, im-, il-, ir-**	*in, into* inspect incision influx
|| **in-, im-, il-, ir-**	*not* incredible intact infidel
incud	*anvil* incus incudiform incudectomy
ind	*Indian* indigo Hindustan Indonesia
indi-	*within* indigenous indigent indigence
indic	*pointer* indication indices index
-ine	*like, related to* masculine bovine saline
infra-	*beneath* infrared infracostal infracortical
insul	*island* insular insulation peninsula
int-	*within* interior internal intestine

integr	*whole*	
	integrity integration integer	
inter-	*between*	
	intercept intermission international	
intra-	see **intro-**	
intro-, intra-	*inside*	
	introduce introvert intramural	
iod, ion	*violet*	
	iodine iodize Ionidium	
|| **-ion, -tion**	*state, quality, act, -ing*	
	action diction graduation	
ion	see **iod**	
ir-	see **in-**	
irid	*rainbow, iris (of eye)*	
	iridescent iris keratoiridocyclitis	
ischi	*hip*	
	ischium ischiocele ischialgia	
-ise	see **-ize**	
-ish	*like, related to*	
	foolish boyish boorish	
-ism	*state, quality, act*	
	dogmatism materialism pantheism	
iso-	*equal*	
	isosceles isometric isothermal	
-ist	*one who*	
	dentist militarist misogynist	
it	*to go*	
	exit transit initiate	
ital	*Italian*	
	italics Italic Italo-American	
-ite	*one who*	
	favorite laborite Semite	
-ite	*related to, having the quality of*	
	dendrite polianite porphyrite	

-itious	*having the quality of* fictitious excrementitious supposititious
-itis	*inflammation* appendicitis arthritis tonsillitis
-ity	*state, quality, act* clarity nobility hilarity
-ium	*chemical element* helium einsteinium europium
-ive	*one who, that which* captive operative missive
-ive	*having the power of* explosive productive counteractive
-ize, -ise	*to make, to act* fertilizer realize revitalize

_J_

jac	see **ject**
jan	*doorway* janitor January Janus
ject, jac	*to throw* reject adjective trajectory
jejun	*fasting, empty* jejune jejunum jejunostomy
joan, john	*God's gracious gift* Joan Joannine John
joc	*joke* jocose juggler jewel
join	see **junct**
journ	*day* journal journey adjourn
jov	*Jove (Jupiter)* jovial Jovian jovicentric

jud	*Jewish* Judaic Judo-Christian Judeophile
jud	*judge* judicious judiciary prejudice
jug	see **junct**
junct, jug, join	*to join, to marry, mating* conjunction junction conjugal
jur	*to swear* juror adjure perjury
juven, jun	*young* juvenile rejuvenate junior
juxta	*next to, beside* juxtapose juxtaposition joust

K

kary, cary	*nucleus, nut* karyosome karyotin caryokinesis
kata-	see **cata-**
kath	see **cath**
ken	see **can**
kerat, cerat	*horn* keratolysis keratoma rhinoceros
keraun	see **ceraun**
ket	*acetone* ketosis ketonuria ketonemia
kilo-, chilio-	*thousand* kilometer kilowatt chiliad
kin	*to beget* kinship kindred kind
-kin	*little, small* napkin manikin Perkins
kine-, cinema-	*to move* kinetic cinema cinematography

klept	*to steal* kleptomaniac kleptophobia biblioklept
know	*to know* knowledge acknowledge known
koni	see **coni**
kre-	see **creat**
kry	see **cry**
krypt	see **crypt**
kym, cym	*wave* kymography kymoscope cymotrichous
kyph	*humpbacked* kyphosis kyphoscoliosis Kyphoclonella

L

la	*people* laity layman Nicholas
lab, lep	*to take, to seize* syllable syllabus epileptic
labi, labr	*lip* labial labiodental labrum
labor	*to work* laborious laboratory Labrador
labr	see **labi**
labyrinth	*maze* labyrinth labyrinthine labyrinthectomy
lac	*milk* lactation lactic lactose
lachrym	see **lacrim**
lack	*loose, to allow* lack slacks lag
lacrim, lachrym	*tear (-drop)* lacrimal lacrimation lachrymose

lacun	*space, hollow* lacuna lacunule Lacunella
laevo-	see **levo-**
laf	*loaf (bread)* loaf lord lady
-lagnia	*lust* osmolagnia coprolagnia pornolagnia
laiss	see **leas**
lal	*to talk, to babble* glossolalia lalopathy Eulalia
lambd	*lambda (λ, Λ), L* lambdoid lambdacism lambdacist
lamell	see **lamin**
lamin, lamell	*leaf, layer* laminated lamellibranch omelet
lan	*wool* lanolin laniferous lanoceric
lanc	*to throw* lance lancet launch
-lani	*heavenly* Leilani Noelani Iwalani
lanthan, lat	*to lie hidden* lanthanum lanthanite latent
lapar	*flank* laparotomy laparocele laparorrhaphy
lapid	*stone* lapidary dilapidated lapidiferous
lapse	*to slip* elapse collapse relapse
larv	*mask, larva* larva larvate larvicide
laryng	*windpipe* laryngitis laryngology laryngectomy

lat	*to carry* translate ventilate legislator
lat	*wide* dilate latitude laticostate
lat	see **lanthan**
later	*side* lateral bilateral laterotorsion
-latry	*worship* idolatory bibliolatry heliolatry
lav, lu	*to wash* lavatory ablution deluge
lax	*loose, to allow* relax laxative languid
leap	*to leap, to run* leap elope gallop
leas, laiss	*loose, to allow* laissez-faire leash lease
lecith	*yolk* lecithin lecithinase lecithal
lect	see **leg**
led	*to lead* leader led load
lef	*to allow, dear* belief love livelong
leg, lig, lect	*to choose, to gather, to read* select eligible illegible
leg	*law* legal legislature legacy
leg	*to lay* lay lie beleaguer
leio-, lio-	*smooth* leiocephalous leiomyosarcoma Liopelmidae
lemm	*skin, rind* lemmocyte neurilemma sarcolemma

leni	*soft, mild* lenient relentless lenitive
lent	*lentil* lens lentiform lenticonus
lent	*slow* lentitude lento lentando
leon	*lion* leonine Leo leontocephalous
lep, lepid	*scale* leper leproma Lepidoptera
lep	see **lab**
lepid	see **lep**
lept	*thin, small* leptosome leptocephaly leptodermous
lern	*to teach* learn learning lore
-less	*without* fearless friendless careless
-let	*little* booklet cutlet bracelet
leth	*death* lethal lethality lethiferous
leth	*to forget* lethargy lethargic Lethe
leuc, leuk	*white* leucocyte leucoderma leukemia
leuk	see **leuc**
lev	*to allow, absence* leave furlough twelve
lev	*light (weight), to raise* alleviate elevator leverage
lev	*smooth* levigation levicellular Levipalifer

levo-, laevo-	*left hand*
	levoversion levorotatory levophobia
lex	*word, speech*
	lexicon lexicology lexicographer
-lexia	*to read*
	bradylexia alexia dyslexia
-ley	*meadow, clearing*
	Stanley Bradley Beverley
liber	*free*
	liberate liberal deliver
liber, libr	*weight, balance*
	deliberate equilibrium lb.
libr	*book*
	library librarian libel
libr	see **liber**
lic	*to entice, to snare*
	elicit delicacy delight
lic	*permissible*
	license illicit licentious
lict	see **linqu**
lid, lis	*to damage*
	collide elide collision
lien	*spleen*
	lienal lienorenal lienocele
lif	*life, to live*
	life lively enliven
lig	*to bind*
	ligament obligation religion
lig	see **leg**
lign	*wood*
	ligneous lignescent lignin
liht	*light*
	light enlighten lightning

lik *similar*
like likeness likewise

limin *threshold*
eliminate preliminary subliminal

limn *pool*
limnology limnobiology limnometer

lin *flax*
linen linoleum linseed

line *line*
lineage delineate patrilineal

-ling *little*
seedling fiingerling fledgeling

lingu *language, tongue*
linguistics bilingual linguopalatal

linqu, lict *to leave*
relinquish delinquent derelict

lio- see **leio-**

lip, lipo- *fat*
glycolipin lipogenetic lipocardiac

lip *to leave, to abandon, to lack*
eclipse elliptical lipogram

lipo- see **lip**

liqu *fluid*
liquid liquor liquidate

lis see **lid**

lit *bed*
litter (bed) litter (offspring) litter (v.)

-lite *stone*
praseolite siderolite physalite

liter *letter*
literal illiterate obliterate

lith *stone*
lithograph monolith paleolithic

littor	*seashore*
	littoral Littorina Littorella
lob	*lobe*
	lobotomy lobulus lobiform
loc	*place*
	local location locomotive
loc	see **loqu**
loft	*air*
	aloft loft lift
log	*word, discourse*
	travelogue monologue eulogy
-logy, -ology	*discourse, study*
	biology geology psychology
long	*long*
	longevity elongate prolong
loqu, loc	*to speak*
	loquacious elocution ventriloquist
los	*to lose*
	loser loss forlorn
lox	*oblique*
	loxodont loxosoma loxodograph
lubr	*slippery*
	lubrication lubricant lubricity
luc	*light*
	lucid translucent lucubrate
lucr	*money, profit*
	lucre lucrative lucrific
luct	*to struggle*
	reluctant ineluctable eluctation
lud, lus	*to play*
	prelude delude collusion
lumb	*loin*
	lumbar lumbago dorsolumbar
lumin	*opening, light*
	lumen luminescence illumination

lun	*moon* lunar lunate lunatic
lup	*wolf* lupine lupicide lupiform
lus	see **lud**
lute	*yellow* luteal luteovirescent luteous
-ly	*having the quality of* manly motherly miserly
-ly	*in the manner of* childishly wickedly erroneously
lyc	*wolf* lycanthropy lycorexia Lycaenidae
lymph	*clear water* lymphatic lymphocyte lymphoma
lys, lyt	*to free* analysis histolytic electrolyte
lyt	see **lys**

M

-ma	*something done* drama stigma diploma
mac, mc	*son of* MacDonald McGregor McDaniel
mac	*thin* emaciated macilent meager
-machy	*battle* sciamachy gigantomachy logomachy
macro-	*big* macron macrocosm macroeconomics
macul	*spot, stain* immaculate maculocerebral macular

mael   *to grind*
                      maelstrom   meal   mellow

mag   *to be able*
                      might   may   dismay

magister   *greater, superior*
                      magistrate   master   mister

magn-   *great*
                      magnify   magnificent   magnate

magnes, magnet   *Magnesia (in Thessaly)*
                      magnesium   magnet   manganese

magnet   see **magnes**

maha-   *great*
                      maharaja   mahatma   maharani

major   *larger*
                      majority   majordomo   mayor

mak   *to make*
                      maker   made   match (v.)

mal   *bad, badly*
                      malformation   maladjusted   dismal

malac   *soft*
                      malacoid   osteomalacia   malacophyllous

malle   *hammer*
                      mallet   malleable   malleolus

mamm   *breast*
                      mammal   mammary   mammiform

man   *gas*
                      manometer   manograph
                      syphgmomanometer

man   *man, human being*
                      manslaughter   woman   manikin

man   *to stay*
                      permanent   mansion   remain

-mancy   *divination*
                      pyromancy   necromancy   chiromancy

mand	*to entrust, to command*
	mandate remand mandatory
mandib	*lower jaw*
	mandible mandibuliform
	mandibulopharyngeal
mania	*craving, insanity*
	maniac monomania pyromania
manu	*hand*
	manufacture manual manacle
mar	*Mars (god)*
	martial Mars (planet) Mardi Gras
mar	*sea*
	maritime submarine marina
margarit	*pearl*
	margaritiferous Margaret margarine
marit	*husband*
	marital marry mariticide
mark	*boundary, sign*
	mark remarkable demarcation
martyr	*witness*
	martyr martyrdom martyrology
-mas	*Mass (ceremony)*
	Christmas Candlemas Michaelmas
mascul	*man*
	masculine emasculate male
mast	*breast*
	mastitis mastoid mastodon
mater	*mother*
	maternal matrimony matron
math	*to learn*
	mathematics polymath chrestomathy
maur	*dark*
	Mauritania Maurice Moorish
maxill	*jaw*
	maxilla maxillofacial maxillodental

maxim	*largest* maximum maxim maximize
maym	*to mutilate* maim mayhem mangle
maz	*breast* amazon mazopathy mazolysis
mc	see **mac**
mechan	*machine* mechanical mechanic mechanism
med	*to attend to* medicine remedy meditate
med	*middle* medium mediator medieval
medull	*marrow* medulla medullary medullo-arthritis
meg-	see **mega-**
mega-, megal-, **meg-**	*great, million* megaphone megalomaniac megohm
megal-	see *mega-*
mel	*apple* melon marmalade chamomile
mel	*limb* phocomelia anisomelia melagra
mel	*song* melody melodrama melophone
melan	*black* melancholy Melanesia calomel
melior	*better* ameliorate meliorant meliorism
mell	*honey* mellifluous molasses marmalade
membr	*limb, member* member dismember membrane

memor
to remember
memory   commemorate   memorandum

men
to lead
promenade   amenable   demeanor

men
moon, month
menopause   menorrhea   menology

-men
something done
specimen   regimen   acumen

men
see **mens**

mend
fault
amendment   emendation   mend

mening
membrane
meningitis   meninges   meningioma

mens
to measure
dimension   immense   commensurate

mens
moon, month
menses   menstruation   mensual

mens
table
mensa   commensal   mesa

ment
chin
mentolabial   mentigerous   mentoposterior

ment
mind
mentality   demented   amentia

-ment
state, quality, act
abasement   excitement   aggrandizement

-ment
that which
inducement   sediment   impediment

mer
to earn
merit   meritorious   meretricious

mer
part
polymerous   isomer   meroblastic

mer
thigh
merosthenic   meralgia   merocele

merc
to trade
merchant   mercenary   market

mercur	*Mercury (god)* mercury mercurial Mercury (planet)
merg, mers	*to dip, to plunge* merger submerge immerse
meridi	*south, noon* meridional meridian a.m.
mers	see **merg**
meso-	*middle* mesoderm mesomorphic Mesopotamia
-mester	*month* semester semestral trimester
met	*to measure, fitting* mete meet (adj.) helpmate
met	*meat, food* meat mate inmate
met	*to meet* meet (v.) meeting moot
met-	see **meta-**
meta-, met-	*beyond, change* metaphor metabolism metamorphosis
meter, metr	*measure* thermometer perimeter asymmetrical
methy	*wine* methyl amethyst methomania
metr	*mother* metropolis metropolitan metropolite
metr	*womb* endometrium metrocele myometrium
metr	see **meter**
mezz	*half* mezzanine mezzo-soprano mezzotint
mi	*less, little* miargyrite Miocene Miohippus

miasm	*pollution*
	miasma miasmic Miastor
micro-	*small*
	microscope microphone microbe
migra	*to wander*
	migration emigrate immigrant
milan	*Milan (Italy)*
	milanaise Milanese milliner
milit	*to fight*
	militant militate militia
milli-	*thousand*
	million millimeter millennium
mim	*to imitate, to copy*
	mimic mimeograph pantomime
min	*less, little*
	diminish minority mince
min	*to project, to hang over*
	prominent imminent menace
minim	*least, smallest*
	minimum minimize minim
minister	*to serve*
	minister administration minstrel
mir	*to wonder*
	admire miracle mirror
mis-	*bad, badly*
	misinform mispronounce misnomer
mis-	*to hate*
	misanthrope misogynist misoneism
misc	*to mix*
	miscellaneous miscegenation
	promiscuous
miser	*wretched*
	miser miserable commiserate
miss	see **mit**

mit, miss	*to send* transmit missile missionary
mit	*thread* mitochondrion mitosis mitoplasm
mitr	*headband* mitral miter mitella
mix	*to mix* mixotrophic apomixis mixobiosis
mne	*to remember* amnesia mnemonics amnesty
mob	see **mov**
mod	*measure, manner* modest mode accommodate
mol	*to grind (grain)* molar immolate emolument
mol	*heap, burden* demolish molecule molest
moll	*soft* mollify mollusk emollient
molybd	*lead (metal)* molybdenum molybdena molybdic
mon	*moon* Monday month monthly
mon-, ma-	*my* monsignor madam mesdames
mong	*to mix* among mongrel mingle
moni	*to advise, to remind* monitor admonish monument
mono-	*one* monogram monologue monolith
• **mont**	see **mount**
-mony	*state, quality, that which* matrimony acrimony alimony

mor	*custom* mores moral amorality
mor	*stupid* moron sophomore morology
morb	*disease* morbid morbigenous morbose
morph	*form* morphology amorphous metamorphosis
mors, mord	*to bite* morsel remorse mordacious
mort	*death* mortuary mortgage mortal
mot	see **mov**
• **mount, mont**	*hill, mountain* surmount paramount Piedmont
-mouth	*mouth (of river)* Portsmouth Monmouth Plymouth
mov, mot, mob	*to move* move motive automobile
muc	*mucus, moldy, sticky* mucoid mucin mucilage
mucedin	*mildew* mucedinous mucedinaceous mucedine
multi-	*many* multiply multilateral multipurpose
mun	*gift, service* remunerate municipal immune
mund	*clean* mundatory mundificant Mundia
mund	*world* mundane mundanity mundivagant
mur	*wall* mural intramural immure
murn	*to grieve* mourn mourning mournful

mus	*mouse, muscle* musophobia muscle musculature
mus	*one of the nine Muses* music museum mosaic
musc	*a fly* muscicide mosquito musket
mut	*to change* mutation immutable commute
my	*mouse, muscle* myomancy myology myoma
myc	*fungus* mycosis mycelium neomycin
myel	*marrow, spinal cord* myelin myelocyte poliomyelitis
myria-	*countless, ten thousand* myriad myriapod myriameter
myring	*membrane, eardrum* myringa myringitis myringoscope
myrmec	*ant* myrmecology myrmecophagous myrmotherine
mys	*pollution* mysophobia mysophobic mysophilia
myst	*mystery* mystify mystagogue mystical
mytil	*mussel* mytilotoxism Mytilus mytilite
myx	*mucus* myxadenitis myxocyte myxedema

<u>N</u>

n-	*not* never neither none
nam	*name* nameless namesake namely

nan	*dwarf*
	nanocephalic nanomelus nannander
nap	*small sheet*
	napkin map apron
nar	see **nas**
narc	*numbness, stupor*
	narcotic narcosynthesis narcissus
nas, nar	*nose*
	nasal nasturtium nares
nasc	see **nat**
nat, nasc	*to be born*
	native nature nascent
nav	*ship, to sail*
	navy navigation nave
naut	*to sail*
	nautical astronaut nausea
ne-	*not*
	nefarious neuter nescient
nec	see **necr-**
necr-, nec	*death, dead*
	necrology necromancy nectar
nect	*to knot*
	connect net annex
nect	*to swim*
	nectopod nectocalyx Necturus
ned	*need*
	needy needless needful
neg	*to deny*
	negative abnegation negotiate
neigh	*near*
	neighbor nigh next
nemat	*thread*
	nematode nemathelminthes nematocyst

neo-	*new* neon neo-Nazi neologism
nephr-	*kidney* nephrology nephritis nephrolith
nepot	*nephew* nephew nepotism niece
neptun	*Neptune (god)* Neptune (planet) neptunium neptunite
nerv	*nerve* nervous enervate. innervate
nes	*island* Polynesia Indonesia Melanesia
-ness	*state, quality* kindness happiness friendliness
neth	*below* nether Netherlands beneath
| **neur**	*nerve* neurology neuralgia neuritis
neutr	*neither* neutral neuter neutroceptor
nickel	*devil, nickel* nickeliferous nickeline nickelous
nictitat	*winking* nictitate nictitation connive
nid	*nest* nidificate nidicolous nidifugous
nigr	*black* Negro negroid denigrate
niht	*night* nightly midnight benighted
-nik	*one who* sputnik beatnik nudnik
nitr	*niter, nitrogen* nitrate nitrous nitrobenzene

niv	*snow* niveous nivicolous Nevada
no	*to know* noble notorious denote
noc, nox	*to injure* nocent innocent innocuous
noc, nox	*night* nocturne nocturnal equinox
nod	*knot* node nodule nodiflorous
nom	*law, order* astronomy economy binomial
nom	see **nomin**
nomin, nom	*name* nomination misnomer nominal
non-	*not* nonsense nonpartisan nonessential
non	see **novem**
nor-	*north* Norway Normandy Norfolk
norm	*a rule* normative abnormal enormous
nos	*disease* nosology nosetiology nosogeography
nos	*nose* nostril nosegay nozzle
noto-	*back (of body)* notochord notopodium Notonecta
noto-	*south* Notopithecus Nototherium Notogean
nounce	see **nunc**
nov	*new* novelty renovate innovation

novem, non	*nine* November novena nonagon
nox	see **noc**
nub, nupt	*to marry* connubial nubile nuptial
nucle	*nut, kernel* nucleus nuclear enucleate
nud	*uncovered* nudiped nudiflorous Nudibranchia
nul	*nothing* nullify annul annulment
numer	*number* numerous numeral enumerate
nunc, nounce	*to announce* enunciate pronounce denounce
nupt	see **nub**
nutri	*to nourish* nutrition nutritive nutriment
nyct	*night* nyctophobia nyctalopia nyctitropic
nymph	*maiden* nymphal nymphlike nympholepsy
nyx	*puncture* pyronyxis scleronyxis Nyxeophilus

O

o'	*grandson of* O'Connor O'Brien O'Malley
ob-, oc-, of-, **op-**	*to, toward, against* object obstacle opposition
obliqu	*oblique* obliquity obliquimeter Obliquaria

obliv	*to forget* oblivion oblivious oblivescence
oc-	see **ob-**
occident	*west, falling* occident occidental occidentalize
occip	*back of head* occipital occiput occipitocervical
ochlo-	*mob* ochlocracy ochlocrat ochlophobia
ochr	*yellow, pale* ocher ochroid Ochroma
-ock	*little* bullock shamrock buttock
oct-	see **octo-**
octo-, oct-	*eight* octopus octave October
ocul	*eye* oculist binoculars monocle
od, hod	*road* odometer exodus method
od	*smell* odor malodorous ozone
od	*song* ode parody rhapsody
-oda	see **-oid**
-ode	see **-oid**
odi	*to hate* odium odious annoy
odont	*tooth* orthodontist periodontist odontalgia
odyn	*pain* anodyne arthrodynia neurodynia
oec	see **eco-**

oen, en	*wine* oenocyte oenophilist enology
of-	see **ob-**
-oid, -oda, -ode	*resembling* spheroid asteroid nematode
oint	see **unct**
ois, es	*to bear, to carry* Oesophagicola Stomoisia esophagus
-ol	see **ole**
ole, -ol	*oil* petroleum oleomargarine cholesterol
olfact	*smelling* olfactory olfaction olfactometer
oligo-	*few* oligophrenia oligarchy oligotrophic
-ology	see **-logy**
olymp	*(Mt.) Olympus* Olympics Olympiad Olympian
-oma	*growth, tumor* carcinoma myoma sarcoma
ombr	*rain* ombrophilous ombrometer ombrifuge
-ome	*group* rhizome caulome mestome
omma, ommat	*eye* ommatophore ommatidium Loxomma
ommat	see **omma**
omni-	*all* omnipotent omnivorous omniscient
omphal	*navel* omphaloskepsis omphalic Choanomphalus
-on	*Greek ending* criterion pantheon phenomenon

onc	*hook* onchium blepharoncus Oncorhyncus
onc	*mass, tumor* oncology nephroncus hematoncometry
onoma	see **onym**
ont	*being* ontology ontogeny sporont
onych	*claw, (finger-)nail* onychauxis leukonychia anonychia
onym, onoma	*name* synonym anonymous onomatopoeia
oö-	*egg* oölogy oögenesis oöcyte
op	*eye, sight* optical optometrist myopic
op-	see **ob-**
oper	*work* operate cooperation opera
opercul	*lid* operculum operculate operculiferous
ophi, ophidi	*snake* ophiology ophidiophobia Ophelia
ophidi	see **ophi**
ophthalm	*eye* ophthalmology ophthalmic ophthalmoscope
opi	*opium* opiate opiomania opiophagous
opistho-	*back* opisthotic opisthodont opisthograph
opl	*weapon* panoply anoplocephalic hoplite
opsi-	*late* opsimath opsiuria opsigamy

opt	*to choose* option adopt co-opt
optim	*best* optimum optimist optimize
or, os	*mouth* oral orifice osculate
-or	*one who, that which* donor curator tractor
ora	*to speak, to pray* oration oracle inexorable
-orama	*view* panorama diorama cinerama
orb	*circle* orb orbit exorbitant
orch	*to dance* orchestra orchestration Orchestia
orchid	*testicle* orchid cryptorchidism orchidectomy
ordin	*order* coordination subordinate ordination
orex	*appetite* anorexia hyperorexia lycorexia
organ	*instrument* organic organization organon
ori, ort	*to rise, to be born* origin aborigine abortive
orient	*east, rising* orient oriental orientation
-orious	*having the quality of* notorious victorious censorious
-orium	see **-ory**
orn	*to decorate* ornate ornament adornment
ornith	*bird* ornithology ornithoscopy ornithophilous

ort	see **ori**
orth-	*straight, right* orthopedics orthodox orthography
-ory	*like, having the quality of* preparatory regulatory promissory
-ory, orium	*place where* factory lavatory auditorium
os	see **or**
oscill	*to swing* oscillate oscilloscope oscillometer
-ose	*having the quality of* jocose verbose bellicose
-osis, -sis	*condition, act* sclerosis cyanosis analysis
osm	*pushing* osmosis osmotic endosmosis
osm	*smell* anosmia osmesthesia osmium
osphr	*smell* osphretic osphradium osphrencephalon
oss	*bone* ossify ossicle osseous
oste	*bone* osteology osteomyelitis osteopath
osti	*door, opening* ostium ostiary ostiole
ostrac	*shell* ostracize entomostracan Ostracoderm
ot	*ear* otology otitis otoscope
oti	*ease* otiose negotiate negotiable
-otic	*having the quality of, related to* neurotic narcotic psychotic

-ous	*having the quality of* slanderous tortuous amorous
out-	*out* outlaw utter utmost
outr-	see **ultra**
ov	*egg* oval ovary oviparous
over-	*above, too much* overdone overwork overextend
-ovna	*daughter of* Alexandrovna Ivanovna Petrovna
-ow	*having the quality of* mellow yellow callow
own	*to have* owner disown ought
oxy	*sharp, acid* oxygen oxide paroxysm

P

pac	*peace* pacifier pacifist Pacific
pachy-	*thick* pachyderm pachyonchia pachynema
pact	*to agree, to fasten* pact compact impact
pag	see **pec**
pal	*pale* pallor pallid appalling
palai	see **pale**
pale, palai	*ancient* paleolithic paleontology palaiotype
pali	see **palin**

palin, pali *back, again*
palindrome palingenesis palinode

pallad *Pallas (Athena)*
Pallas (planetoid) palladium palladous

palli *mantle, cloak*
palliate pallium palliative

palp *to pat, feeler*
palpable palpate palpulus

pan-, panto- *all*
panorama pantheon pantomime

pan *bread*
pantry company companion

pan *small cloth*
pane panel impanel

panto- see **pan-**

pap, pop *father*
papa papal pope

papilion *butterfly*
papilionid papilionaceous pavilion

papill *nipple*
papilla papilloma papillectomy

par *to appear*
apparent apparition appearance

par, part *to bear*
parent viviparous parturition

par *equal*
parity compare disparage

par *to prepare*
pare apparatus separate

par- see **para-**

para-, par- *beside, variation*
paradox parathyroid parenthesis

para *to prevent*
parachute parasol parapet

pariet	*wall*
	parietal parietitis parietofrontal
parl	*word, speech*
	parley parlor parole
part	*part*
	participate particolored particle
part	see **par**
parthen	*virgin*
	parthenon parthenogenesis parthenospore
parv	*small*
	parvity parvule parvicellular
pass	see **pat**
past	*dough*
	paste pastry pastel
past	*to feed*
	pasture pastor repast
pat, pass	*to lie open*
	patent (adj.) passage patent (v.)
pat, pass	*to suffer*
	patient passive compassion
patell	*pan, dish*
	patella patelliform patellofemoral
pater	*father*
	paternal patriot repatriation
path	*feeling, suffering, disease*
	apathy sympathetic pathology
path	*path*
	pathway footpath pathfinder
patul	*spread*
	patulous patulent Patulaxis
pauci-	*few*
	paucity pauciloquy paucifoliate
paul	*little*
	Paul Paulocrinus Pauloscirtes

paul *pause*
paulospore paulocardia Paulomagus

paus *to cease*
pause menopause diapause

pec, pex, pag *to fasten*
pectin hepatopexy thoracopagus

pectin *comb*
pectinate pectiniform pectineal

pector *chest*
pectoral expectorate pectoriloquy

pecu *money, cattle, property*
pecuniary impecunious peculation

ped *child*
pediatrician pedagogue orthopedist

ped *foot*
pedal pedestrian impede

ped *ground*
pedology pedograph pedogeography

pedicul *louse*
pediculosis pediculicide pediculophobia

pel, puls *to push*
propel expulsion repulsive

pel *skin*
pelt pellagra surplice

pel- see **per-**

pelag *sea*
archipelago pelagic bathypelagic

pelecy *hatchet*
pelecoid Pelecypoda Pelecystoma

pelv *basin*
pelvis pelvic pelviform

pen *almost*
peninsula penultimate peneplain

pen *punishment*
penalty penance repent

pen	*tail, penis* pencil Penicillium penicillin
pend, pens	*to hang, to weigh, to pay* pendulum pensive compensation
-penia	*to need, to lack* thrombopenia erythrocytopenia eosinopenia
penn	see **pinn**
pens	see **pend**
penta-	*five* pentagon pentameter pentathlon
peps	see **pept**
pept, peps	*to digest* peptic dyspepsia eupeptic
‖ **per-, pel-**	*through, intensive* permit perspire pellucid
per	*to try out* experience expert peril
perei	*to transport* pereiopod pereion Pereionotus
peri-	*around* periscope perimeter perigee
persic	*Persian* Persic Persicaria peach
pest	*plague* pest pestilence pestiferous
petal	*leaf, thin plate* petal petalite petalodont
petit	*to seek* petition competitor appetite
petit	*small, little* petite petticoat petty
petr	*rock* petroleum petrify Peter

pex	see **pec**
pha	see **phe**
phac, phak	*lentil, lens* phacolith phacosclerosis phakitis
phag	*to eat* sarcophagus esophagus anthropophagous
phalang	*in ranks* phalanx phalange brachyphalangia
phall	*penis* phallus phallic phalloid
phan, phen	*to show, to appear* diaphanous phantom phenomenon
phaner	*visible* phanerocryst phanerogam phaneroscopy
pharmac	*drug* pharmacy pharmacist pharmaceutical
pharyng	*throat* pharyngeal pharyngitis pharyngectomy
phas	see **phe**
phe, phas	*to say, to speak* prophesy euphemism aphasia
phen	see **phan**
pher	see **phor**
phil	*to love* philanthropist philosopher Philadelphia
phleb	*vein* phlebitis phlebology phlebotomy
phlegm	*flame* phlegm phlegmatic adenophlegmon
phlog	*flame* phlogiston antiphlogistic phlogocytosis
phob	*to fear* claustrophobia acrophobia hydrophobia

phoc	*seal (animal)* phocine phocomelia Phocodontia
phoenic	*red* phoenix phoenicite Phoenicopterus
phon	*sound* phonograph telephone cacophony
phor, pher	*to carry* phosphorus semaphore Christopher
phos	see **phot**
phot, phos	*light* photograph photosynthesis phosphorus
phragm, phrax	*fence, enclosure* diaphragm phragmoplast emphraxis
phras	*speech* phrase phraseology periphrasis
phren	*brain* phrenology schizophrenic frantic
phthis	*to waste away* phthisic ophthalmophthisis phthisiology
phthong	*voice, sound* diphthong phthongometer aphthongia
phyl	*tribe, race, phylum* phylum phylogeny Phylarchus
phylac	*guard* prophylactic anaphylaxis phylactery
phyll	*leaf* chlorophyll phyllophagous phyllopod
phym	*growth* phymatosis arthrophyma phymatodes
phys	*bellows, bladder* physocele emphysema physalite
physi	*nature, natural* physics physiology physique
phyt	*plant* phytology neophyte phytogenesis

pi	*holy, tender* pious pity *pia mater*
picr	*bitter* picrodendron picrite chloropicrin
pict	*to paint* picture depict pigment
pil	*ball* pill pellet piles
pil	*hair* depilatory caterpillar pillage
pin	*pine cone* pineal pinoid pinetum
pinn, pinnat, penn	*feather* pinniform pinnatiped pennoplume
pinnat	see **pinn**
pisc	*fish* piscatorial piscine Pisces
pithec	*ape* cercopithecus Pithecanthropus Australopithecus
pituit	*phlegm* pituitary pituitous pituicyte
plac	*flat* placodont placoderm placoplast
plac	*to please* placid implacable complacent
placent	*flat cake* placenta extraplacental placentoid
plagi	*oblique* plagioclase plagiocephalic plagiograph
plain	*to lament* complain plaintive plaintiff
plan	*flat, soft (sound)* plain plane piano

plan	*to wander* planet aplanobacter planogamete
plant	*sole of the foot* planta plantar plantigrade
• **plas**	*to form* plastic plaster protoplasm
platin	*silver, platinum* platinum platiniridium platinate
platy-	*flat, broad* platypus platyhelminth platyrrhine
plaud	*to strike, to applaud* plaudit plausible explode
-ple	*-fold, times* triple quadruple multiple
ple, plei	*more* pleonasm pleodont pleiomery
pleb	*people* plebiscite plebeian plebicolar
plect	*twisted* Plectanella Plectaster Plectognathi
pleg	*stroke, paralysis* hemiplegia paraplegia plegometer
plei	see **ple**
plen, plet, -ply	*full* plenitude complete supply
pless	see **plex**
plet	see **plen**
pleth	*full* plethora plethysmograph Plethodon
pleur	*side, rib* pleurisy pleurodont pleuroperitoneum
plex, plic, -ply	*to fold* complex explicit multiply

plex, pless	*to strike*
	apoplexy pleximeter plessigraph
plic	see **plex**
| **plor**	*to cry*
	implore deplore explore
plum	*feather*
	plume plumage plumiped
plumb	*lead (metal), plumb-line*
	plumber plumb plummet
plur	see **plus**
plus, plur	*more*
	plus surplus plurality
plut	*Pluto (god)*
	Pluto (planet) plutonium plutonic
plut	*wealth*
	plutocrat plutocracy plutology
pluvi	*rain*
	pluviometer pluvial plover
-ply	see **plen**
-ply	see **plex**
pne	see **pneumon**
pneumon,	*to breathe, lung*
pneum, pne	pneumonia pneumatic traumatopnea
pock	*sack*
	pocket pockmark pouch
pod, pus	*foot*
	tripod chiropodist octopus
poe	see **poie**
pogon	*beard*
	pogonology pogoniasis Calopogon
poie, poe	*to make, to produce*
	sarcopoietic hematopoiesis poet
pol	*axis of a sphere*
	pole polar peripolar

pol	*to polish* polish polite politesse
pol	*Polish* polonaise polonium polka
poli, polit	*city, state* politics polity police
poli	*gray* poliomyelitis polianite Polianthes
-polis	*city* metropolis cosmopolitan Annapolis
polit	see **poli**
poll	*head* poll polls tadpole
poly-	*many* polygon polytheism polygamy
poly	*to sell* monopoly monopolistic oligopoly
pom	*fruit, apple* pomiferous pommel pomegranate
pon, pos	*to place, to put* postpone deposit proposition
ponder	*weight* ponder ponderous preponderant
pont	*bridge* pontoon pontocerebellar pontiff
pop	see **pap**
popul	*people* population populace popular
por	*callus* porocele porokeratosis porosis
por	*opening, passage* pore porous blastopore
porn	*prostitute* pornography pornocracy pornolagnia

porphyr *violet*
porphyry   porphyrin   porphyrogen

port *to carry*
report   transportation   deportee

port *harbor, gate*
port   portal   opportune

pos see **pon**

pos see **pot**

poss see **pot**

post- *after*
postpone   post-mortem   posthumous

poster- *behind, after*
posterior   posterity   preposterous

pot, poss *to be able*
potent   potentate   possible

pot, pos *to drink*
potion   symposium   poison

potam *river*
hippopotamus   potamology   Mesopotamia

potass *potash, potassium*
potassium   potassic   potassamide

poul *chicken*
poultry   pullet   polecat

-poulos *son of*
Constantinopoulos   Giannopoulos
Georgiopoulos

pract, prax *to do*
practical   apraxia   pragmatic

prae- see **pre-**

pras *green*
praseodymium   praseolite   prasine

prav *crooked*
depraved   depravity   depravation

prax see **pract**

pre-, prae-	*before* preview predict praesidium
prec	*to pray* imprecate deprecate precarious
preci	*price* precious appreciate depreciate
pred	*booty* predatory depredation prey
prehend, **prehens, pris**	*to take, to seize* comprehend apprehension prison
prehens	see **prehend**
presby	*old* presbyophrenia presbyopia Presbyterian
press, print	*to press* impress depression reprint
preter-	*beyond* preternatural preterite pretermission
prim, prin	*first* primary primitive principal
prin	see **prim**
print	see **press**
pris	see **prehend**
priv	*single, separate* private privilege deprive
pro-	*for, before, forward* program provision progress
prob	*to test, good* probation approbation prove
proct	*anus* proctology proctodynia periproct
prol	*offspring* prolific proliferate proletariat
prometh	*Prometheus (Greek hero), provident* Promethean promethium Promethichthys

propr	one's own
	proprietor property appropriate
pros-	front, forward
	prosopyle prosenchyma prosthermotaxis
prosop	face
	diprosopus prosopalgia Prosopothrips
proto-	first
	proton prototype protozoa
prox	near
	proximity approximate proximal
pseud	false
	pseudonym pseudoscience pseudopod
psor	itch
	psoriasis psorosperm Psoraphora
psych	mind
	psychology psychiatry psychosomatic
psychr	cold
	psychrometer psychrograph psychrophilic
pter	feather, wing
	pterodactyl helicopter pterosaur
pterid	fern
	pteridophyte pteridography pteridoid
pto	to fall
	ptomaine symptom nephroptosis
ptyal	spittle
	ptyalism ptyalin ptyalocele
pub	mature, pubic
	puberty pubescent pubofemoral
pud	to be ashamed, to be modest
	impudent pudent pudenda
pugn	to fight
	pugnacious repugnant pygmy
pulchr	beauty
	pulchritude pulchritudinous pulchrify

pulm, pulmon	*lung* pulmonary pulmolith pulmotor
pulmon	see **pulm**
puls	see **pel**
pulver	*dust* pulverize pulvereous powder
pulvin	*cushion* pulvinus pulvinate pulvillus
pun	*to punish* punish punitive impunity
punct	see **pung**
pung, punct	*to prick* pungent puncture compunction
pupa	*doll, child* puppet pupil pupa
pur	*clean* pure purify purification
pur, pus	*foul matter* purulent suppurate pustule
purg	*to clean* purge purgative unexpurgated
purpur	*purple* purpura purpurogenous purpurescent
pus	see **pod**
pus	see **pur**
put	*to prune, to correct* amputate impute compute
putr	*rotten* putrid putrescent putrefaction
py	*pus* pyorrhea pyosis pyemia
pycn	*thick* pycnic pycnometer Pycnogonida

pyel	*trough, basin*
	pyelometry pyelogram nephropyelitis
pyg	*buttocks*
	callipygian steatopygous Macropygia
pyl	*gate*
	pylorus micropyle pylangium
pyr	*fire*
	pyromaniac pyrotechnics pyrography
pyr	*pear*
	pyriform Pyrola Pyroplasma
pyren	*fruit-stone*
	pyrenoid pyrenolysis pyrenocarp
pyret	*fever*
	pyretogenesis antipyretic pyretetiology

Q

quadr-, quart	*four*
	quadruplets quadrangle quarter
qual	*what kind*
	quality qualify qualifications
quant	*how much*
	quantity quantitative quantum
quart	see **quadr-**
quer	*to complain*
	querulous quarrel querimonious
quest, quir, quis	*to ask, to seek*
	question inquire inquisitive
quies, quiet	*to rest*
	acquiesce quiet acquit
quiet	see **quies**
quinqu-, quint-	*five*
	quintuplets quintet quintessence
quint-	see **quinqu-**

quir	see **quest**
quot	*how many* quota quotient quotennial

R

rab	*rabies* rabid rabigenic rabiform
rach, rrhach	*spine* rachitic rachiodont hematorrhachis
rad	*ray* radiation radium radius
rad	see **ras**
radic	*root* radical eradicate radish
ram	*branch* ramification ramiform ramigerous
ran	*frog* ranunculus ranine Ranidae
rap	*to snatch, to seize* rapid rapacity rape
raph, raphid, -rrhaph	*to sew, suture* raphides rhapsody gastrorrhaphy
raphid	see **raph**
ras, rad	*to scrape* erase abrasive abrade
rat	*to reckon, to reason* rational ratify ratio
re-	*back, again* report retract recurrent
re	*thing* republic real reify
rec	*to stretch* reach overreach rack

reck   *to heed*
reckon   reckoning   reckless

rect   *to rule, straight, right*
rector   direct   rectify

red   *to interpret*
read   reader   riddle

red   *red*
redden   ruddy   rusty

reg   *to rule, straight, right*
regime   region   regulate

rem   *oar*
trireme   quinquereme   remiform

ren   *kidney*
renal   adrenalin   renoparietal

rept   *to creep*
reptile   reptant   surreptitious

ret   *net*
retothelium   retina   reticulate

retro-   *backwards*
retrogression   retrospect   retroactive

rev   see **rob**

rhabd   *rod*
rhabdocoele   rhabdolith   rhabdomancy

rhen   *Rhine (River)*
Rhenish   rhenium   Rhineland

rhin   *nose*
rhinoceros   rhinitis   rhinoscope

rhiz   *root*
rhizopod   hydrorhiza   rhizophagous

rhod   *red*
rhododendron   rhodium   Rhode Island

rhomb   *to spin*
rhombus   rhomboid   rhombiform

rhynch   *snout*
                     rhynchophorous   rhyncholite
                     Trypanorhyncha

rhyt, rut   *wrinkle*
                     rhytidome   rhytidectomy   rutidosis

rhythm   *measured flow*
                     rhythmic   rhythmometer   rhyme

rid, ris   *to laugh*
                     ridiculous   deride   derision

rid   *to ride*
                     rider   road   raider

rip, riv   *(river-)bank*
                     riparian   rival   derivation

ripe   *ripe*
                     ripen   reap   reaper

ris   *to rise*
                     arise   raise   rouse

ris   see **rid**

-rix, -trix   *feminine*
                     aviatrix   mediatrix   executrix

ro   *fame*
                     Robert   Roger   Roland

rob   *oak, strong*
                     robust   corroboration   corroborative

rob, rev   *to rob, booty*
                     robbery   robe   bereave

rode, ros   *to gnaw*
                     rodent   corrode   erosion

rog   *to ask*
                     interrogate   prerogative   arrogant

roll, rol   *to roll*
                     role   controller   roulette

roman   *Roman*
                     romance   romaine   Rumania

ros	*rose, red*
	rosaceous rosy rosary
ros	see **rode**
rost	*gridiron*
	roster roast roaster
rostr	*beak, prow*
	rostrum rostrate rostellum
rot	*wheel, to turn*
	rotate rotary rotund
rrhach	see **rach**
-rrhage, -rrhex	*to burst, to flow*
	hemorrhage menorrhagia
	metrorrhexis
-rrhaph	see **raph**
-rrhea	*to flow*
	pyorrhea diarrhea logorrhea
-rrhex	see **-rrhage**
rub	*red*
	ruby rubella rubric
rud	*crude*
	rude erudition rudimentary
ruf	*red*
	rufous ruficaudate Rufus
rug	*wrinkle*
	rugate ruga Rugaceae
rugh	*shaggy*
	rough rug ragged
run	*to run*
	outrun runway runaround
rupt	*to break*
	interrupt abrupt rupture
rur	see **rus**
rus, rur	*country*

russ	*Russia*
	Russo-Japanese Russophile Russophobe
rut	see **rhyt**
ruthen	*Russia*
	ruthenium ruthenic Ruthenia
rutil	*red, orange*
	rutilant rutile rutin
-ry	see **-ery**

S

-s	*son of*
	Roberts Williams Jones
sac	*bag*
	sac sack satchel
sacchar	*sugar*
	saccharine saccharic sacchariferous
sacr	*sacred*
	sacrifice sacrilege sacrosanct
sal, sil, sult	*to leap*
	salient resilient insult
sal	*salt*
	saline salinometer salary
salic	*willow*
	salicylic salicetum salicin
salping	*tube, trumpet*
	salpingitis salpingectomy salpingopexy
salut	*health*
	salutary salute salutation
salv	*safe*
	salvation salvage savior
san	*healthy*
	sane sanitary sanitarium

san, sant	*saint, holy* San Francisco Santa Clara Santa Claus
sanct	*holy* sanctify sanctuary sanctimonious
sanguin	*blood* sanguine sanguinary consanguinity
sant	see **san**
sap	*soap* saponaceous saponify soap
sap	*taste, judgment* homo sapiens savor insipid
sapr	*putrid* sapremia saprophyte saprozoic
sarc	*flesh* sarcophagus sarcoma sarcastic
sardin	*Sardinia* sardine sardonic Sardinian
sat	*enough* satisfy saturate insatiable
saturn	*Saturn (god)* saturnine Saturday sapphire
saur	*lizard* dinosaur ichthyosaurus sauropod
sax	*rock* saxifrage saxigenous Saxicola
sax	*(made by Adolphe) Sax* saxophone saxhorn saxtuba
say	*to declare* saying sage saw (proverb)
scala	*ladder* scalar escalator escalation
scand	*Scandinavia* Scandia Scandian scandium
scandal	*stumbling-block* scandalous scandalize slander

scaph	*hollow, boat* scaphoid scaphocephaly Scaphella
scapul	*shoulder blade* scapular scapulet scapulo-clavicular
scat, skat	*dung* scatological scatophilia skatole
scel	*dry* Sceletomerus Sceliphron skeleton
scel	*leg* isosceles scelotyrbe Scelidosaurus
scen	*(stage-) set* proscenium scenario scene
scend, scens, scent	*to climb* descend condescension ascent
scens	see **scend**
scent	see **scend**
schemat	*form, figure* schematic schematograph scheme
schis	see **schiz**
schiz, schis	*to split* schizophrenia schism schist
schol	*leisure* scholar scholastic school
sci	*to know* science omniscient conscious
sci, ski	*shadow* sciamachy skiameter squirrel
sciat	*hip* sciatic sciatica sciatical
scintill	*spark* scintilla scintillating scintillometer
scirrh	*hard* scirrhoid scirrhogastria mastoscirrhus

scler	*hard* sclerosis scleroid scleroderma
scolec	*worm* scolex scoleciasis scolecoidectomy
scoli	*crooked* scoliosis scoliometer scolion
scop	*to look* microscope telescope cystoscope
scor	*notch* score (n.) score (v.) score (twenty)
scot	*darkness* scotopic scototherapy scotophobia
scrap	*to scrape* scraper scrap scramble
scrib, script	*to write* prescribe inscription manuscript
script	see **scrib**
sculp	*to carve* sculptor sculpture scalpel
scut	*shield* scutiform scutate squire
scyph	*cup* scyphus scyphozoan scyphistoma
se-	*apart* secure secluded segregation
seb	*fat* sebaceous sebum seborrhea
sebast	*honored* Sebastopol Sebastian Sebastichthys
sec	see **sect**
sec	see **sequ**
sec	see **sicc**
sect, sec	*to cut* dissect intersection secant

sed, sid, sess	*to sit* sedentary preside session
see	*to see* unforeseen overseer sight
seism	*to shake* seismology seismograph tachyseism
selen	*moon* selenium selenology selenophobia
sell	*to sell* seller sold sale
sem	*sign, meaning* semaphore semantics semeiography
semi-	*half* semiannual semifinal semiconscious
semin	*seed* seminal dissemination seminar
sen	*old* senior senile senator
-sen	see **-son**
sens, sent	*to feel* sensation sensitive sentiment
sent	see **sens**
seps, sept	*putrid* asepsis antiseptic septicemia
sept-	*seven* septennial September septet
sept	*wall* septum septobranch septonasal
sept	see **seps**
septentrion	*north* septentrion septentrional septentrionaline
sequ, sec	*to follow* consequence sequence persecute

ser	*series*
	serial insert dissertation
ser	*watery fluid*
	serum serology seroculture
seric	*silk*
	sericeous sericiculture sericite
serr	see **serrat**
serrat, serr	*a saw*
	serrated serrate Serricornia
serv	*to serv*
	service servile subservient
sesqui	*one-and-one-half*
	sesquicentennial sesquipedalian sesquiquadrate
sess	see **sed**
set	*bristle*
	seta setobranch setaceous
set	see **sit**
sever	*serious*
	severe persevere asseverate
-sex	*Saxon*
	Sussex Wessex Middlesex
sex-	*six*
	sextet sextant siesta
shad	*shade*
	shady shadow shed (n.)
shake	*to shake*
	shaky shock Shakespeare
shape	*form*
	shapely misshapen leadership
shear, shor	*to cut, to divide*
	shears plowshare shore
shin	*to shine*
	shiny shone shimmer

| **-ship** | *state, quality* |
| | hardship   friendship   partnership |

| **shire** | *county* |
| | sheriff   Shropshire   Cheshire |

| **shor** | see **shear** |

| **shot** | *to shoot, to throw* |
| | shoot (v., n.)   shut   sheet |

| **show** | *to look at* |
| | show   showy   sheen |

| **shrub** | *bush* |
| | shrub   shrubbery   scrub (adj.) |

| **shuf** | *to push* |
| | shove   shovel   shuffle |

| **sial** | *saliva* |
| | polysialia   sialolith   sialogram |

| **sib** | *relative* |
| | sibling   sibmate (n., v.)   gossip |

| **sicc, sec** | *dry* |
| | desiccate   siccative   demi-sec |

| **sid** | see **sed** |

| **side** | *side* |
| | besides   sideways   inside |

| **sider** | *iron* |
| | siderolite   siderosis   siderocyte |

| **sider** | *star* |
| | sidereal   sideromancy   siderostat |

| **sigm** | *like a sigma (S), related to sigma* |
| | sigmoid   sigmodont   sigmatic |

| **sign** | *sign* |
| | signal   designate   resignation |

| **sil** | see **sal** |

| **silic** | *flint, silicon* |
| | silicone   silica   siliceous |

silv, sylv	*forest* silvan Pennsylvania savage
sim	*snub-nosed* simian Simobison Simosaur
simil	*like* similar simile assimilate
sin	*Chinese* sinology Sinanthropus Sino-European
sine	*without* sinecure *sine qua non* *sine die*
sing	*to sing* singer sang songstress
sinistr	*left hand* sinister sinistral sinistrorse
sinu	see **sinus**
sinus, sinu	*hollow, curve* sinus sinuous sinupalliate
siphon	*tube* siphon siphonophore siphonostele
-sis	see **-osis**
sist	*to stand, to set* resistant consistency persist
sit, siti	*food, grain* parasite sitology sitiomania
sit, set	*to sit, to set* sitting settee settlement
siti	see **sit**
skat	see **scat**
skep	*to look at, to examine* skeptic omphaloskepsis skepticism
ski	see **sci**
sla	*to strike, to slay* slayer slaughter sly

slav	*Slavic* Slavo-Germanic Slavophile slave
slid	*to slide* slid slither sled
slip	*to glide* slip slippers slippery
slow	*slow* slowly sloth slothful
smith	*worker* blacksmith locksmith wordsmith
snak	*to creep* snake sneak snail
soci	*companion* society association dissociate
sod	*soda, sodium* sodic sodalite sodiohydric
sol	*alone* solo sole solitary
sol	*flat ground* sole (of foot) sole (fish) soil (ground)
sol	*sun* solar solarium solstice
solen	*pipe, channel* solenoid solenoglyph typhlosole
solid	*solid* consolidate solder soldier
solu	see **solv**
solv, solu	*to free* solvent resolve solution
som, somat	*body* chromosome psychosomatic somatogenic
somat	see **som**
-some	*having the quality of* worrisome burdensome lonesome

somn	*sleep*
	somnolent insomnia somnambulist
-son, -sen	*son of*
	Anderson Richardson Hansen
son	*sound*
	resonance unison dissonant
soph	*wise*
	sophomore philosopher sophisticated
sor	*painful*
	sore soreness sorry
soror	*sister*
	sorority sororicide sororiation
sort	*lot, chance*
	consort assortment sorcery
soter	*safety, salvation*
	soteriology soterial creosote
soth	*true*
	soothsayer forsooth soothe
sour	*sour*
	sourdough sauerkraut sorrel (plant)
span	see **hispan**
spasm	*convulsion*
	spasm spasmodic spastic
spec, spic	*to look*
	spectator inspector perspicacity
spek	*to speak*
	speaker speech spoke
spel	*cave*
	speleology spelunker speleothem
spell	*to recite*
	spell (magic) spell (v.) gospel
sper	*to hope*
	desperate despair prosper

sperm, spermat	*seed* spermatozoon spermatogenesis spermatophyte
spermat	see **sperm**
spers	*to strew* aspersion disperse sparse
sphen	*wedge* sphenoid disphenoid sphenogram
spher	*ball* hemisphere spheroid spherical
sphincter	*band* sphincter sphincteral sphincteroplasty
sphing, sphinx	*to bind* sphinx sphingometer sphingiform
sphygm	*pulse* asphyxiate sphygmomanometer sphygmograph
spic	see **spec**
spin	*to spin* spindle spinster spider
spin	*thorn, spine* spiny cerebrospinal porcupine
spir	*breath, life* spirit perspire inspiration
spir	*a coil* spiral aspirin spirochete
splanchn	*viscera* splanchnic splanchnolith splanchnocele
splen	*spleen* splenic splenomegaly hypersplenia
splend	*to shine* splendid splendor resplendent
spond, spons	*to pledge* respond sponsor spouse

spondyl   *vertebra*
spondylotherapy   spondylopathy
Paleospondylus

spong   *sponge*
spongiculture   spongophore
neurospongium

spons   see **spond**

spor   *to sow, seed*
spore   sporadic   sporophyte

|spuri   *false*
spurious   spuriae   Spuriostyloptera

squam   *scale*
squamous   squama   squamoparietal

sta, stit   *to stand, to set*
stable   status   constitution

stagn   *pool*
stagnant   stagnate   tank

stal   see **stol**

stalagm, stalact   *dripping*
stalagmite   stalactite   stalactiform

stall   *place*
pedestal   forestall   installment

-stan   *country*
Pakistan   Afghanistan   Hindustan

stan   see **ston**

stann   *tin*
stannum   stannous   stannic

staped   *stirrup-bone*
stapediform   stapedectomy   stapes

staphyl   *bunch of grapes*
staphylococcus   staphylodermatitis
staphylectomy

star   *stiff, to die*
stare   starve   stern (adj.)

stasis, stat	*standing* prostate hemostat thermostat
stead	*place* steadfast homestead Hampstead
stear	see **steat**
steat, stear	*fat* steatopygous stearic stearate
steg	*roof, covering* stegosaurus branchiostegal Stegocephalia
-stein	*stone* Edelstein Goldstein Silverstein
stell	*star* stellar constellation stellate
sten	*narrow* stenographer stenotopic stenosis
-ster	*one who, woman who* teamster prankster Baxter
ster	*to steer* steerage astern starboard
ster	see **stereo-**
sterc	*dung* stercoral stercoraceous stercorite
stereo-, ster	*three-dimensional, solid* stereophony stereotype cholesterol
stern	*chest, breast* sternum sternotomy sternocostal
steth	*chest, breast* stethoscope stethometer stethophone
sthen	*strong* calisthenics asthenic neurasthenic
sti	*to go up* stirrup stile stair
stib	*mark, antimony* stibium stibnite stibine

stich	*line* hemistich distich acrostic
stig, sting, stinct	*to prick, to mark* instigate stigma distinction
stik	*to pierce* stick stitch sting
stil	*a drop* distil distillery instil
stinct	see **stig**
sting	see **stig**
stip	*to press together* constipate stipulate stevedor
stip	*stem* stipe stipule stipuliferous
stir	*to disturb* stir bestir stormy
stirp	*stem, stock* stirps stirpiculture extirpate
stit	see **sta**
-stle	see **stol**
stol, stal, -stle	*to send* systole peristalsis apostle
stom	*mouth, opening* stomach Chrysostom colostomy
ston, stan	*stone* stony Stanley Stanford
stor	*to set up* store restoration restaurant
strat	*army* strategy stratagem stratocracy
strat	*to spread* prostrate stratification street
strec	*to stretch, to extend* stretcher straight straggler

streph	see **stroph**
strept	see **stroph**
stria	*channel* stria striated striation
strict	see **string**
string, strict	*to tie* stringent district constriction
strobil	*twisted, pine cone* stroboscope strobila strobiliferous
stront	*Strontian (in Scotland), strontium* strontia strontian strontianite
stroph, streph, **strept**	*to turn* catastrophe strephosymbolia streptococcus
struct	*to build* structure obstruct instruction
stult	*stupid* stultify stultiloquence stolid
stup	*struck dumb* stupor stupid stupendous
sty	*enclosure* pigsty steward Stuart
styl	*column, pen* styloglossus peristyle stylus
su-	*south* Sussex Surrey Suffolk
suad, suas	*to advise, to persuade* persuade dissuade suasion
suas	see **suad**
suav	*sweet, agreeable* suave assuage sweet
sub-, suc-, suf-, **sug-, sup-, sur-**	*under* submarine supposition surreptitious
suc-	see **sub-**

sud	*sweat* sudatory sudatorium sudarium
suf-	see **sub-**
sug-	see **sub-**
sui	*self* suicide suicidal *sui generis*
sulc	*furrow* sulcus sulciform sulcate
sulf, sulph	*sulfur* sulfate sulphuric Solferino
sulph	see **sulf**
sult	see **sal**
sum, sumpt	*to take* presume resume consumption
summ	*highest point, sum* summarize summit consummation
sumpt	see **sum**
sup-	see **sub-**
super-, supra-, sur-	*over, above* superior suprarenal survive
supra-	see **super-**
sur-	see **sub-**
sur-	see **super-**
swer	*to swear* answer forswear sworn
swet	*sweet* sweeten sweetheart sweetmeat
sy-	see **syn-**
syl-	see **syn-**
sylv	see **silv**
sym-	see **syn-**

syn-, syl-, sym-,	*with, together*
sys-, sy-	synchronization sympathy systole
syring	*pipe*
	syringe syringium syringomyelia
sys-	see **syn-**

T

ta	see **ton**
tab	*wasting*
	tabes tabescent taboparalysis
tabl	*plank*
	table tablet tabulate
tac, tic	*silent*
	tacit taciturn reticent
tach	*fast*
	tachycardia tachometer tachistoscope
tact	see **tang**
tact	see **tax**
taen	*ribbon, tapeworm*
	taenia taeniasis taeniola
tail	*to cut*
	detail retail tailor
tain	see **ten**
tal	*ankle*
	talipes talotibial talon
tal	see **dal**
tal	see **tell**
tang, tact	*to touch*
	tangible intact contact
tann	*tanbark*
	tan tannic tawny

tantal	*(King) Tantalus* tantalize tantalum tantalus
tapet	*carpet* tapetum tapetal tapesium
taph	*tomb* epitaph cenotaph taphephobia
tard	*late, slow* tardy retard retardation
tars	*instep, (edge of) eyelid* tarsus metatarsal tarsoplasty
taur	*bull* tauromachy Minotaur toreador
tauto-	*same* tautology tautonym tautomerism
tax, tact	*arrangement* syntax taxidermist tactics
tech	*to show, to guide* teach taught token
techn	*art, skill* technology technique pyrotechnic
tect	*builder* architect architectonic tectology
tect	see **teg**
-teen	*and ten* thirteen fifteen nineteen
teg, tect	*to cover* protege protect detective
tele, teli, telo	*end, completion* teleology teliospore telophase
tele-	*from afar* television telephone telemetric
teli	see **tele**
tell, tal	*to count, to relate* teller tale talk

tellur	*earth, tellurium* telluric tellurous telluriferous
telo	see **tele**
temper	*proper mixture* temperate temperance temper (n., v.)
tempor	*time* temporary contemporary temporize
tempt	*to try* tempt attempt tentative
ten, tin, tain	*to hold* tenacious abstinence retain
ten, tenon	*stretched tight* tenodynia tenonitis tenontagra
ten	*ten* tenth fifteenth tithe
tend, tens, tent	*to stretch* tendency extensive attention
tens	see **tend**
tent	see **tend**
tenu	*thin* tenuous attenuate extenuating
ter	*three* ternary tertiary tertian
terat	*monster* teratism teratology teratoma
terg	*back (of body)* tergiversation tergum tergal
term	see **termin**
termin, term	*end, limit* terminal determine exterminate
terr	*earth* territory Mediterranean terrier
terr	*to frighten* terror terrify deterrent

tes	*to pluck* tease tousle tussle
test	*testicle* testitis testibrachium testicond
test	*witness* testify testament protest
tetan	see **ton**
tetra-	*four* tetragon tetrameter tetrasyllabic
text	*to weave* text texture textile
-th	*state, quality, that which* health truth birth
thalam	*(inner) chamber* thalamus hypothalamus thalamencephalon
thalass, thalatt	*sea* thalassiophyte thalassiarch thalattology
thalatt	see **thalass**
thall	*twig, thallium* thalloid thallophyte thalliferous
than	see **thanat**
thanat, than	*death* thanatopsis thanatophobia euthanasia
thaum	*miracle* thaumaturge thaumatology thaumotrope
the, theo	*God* theology atheist Theodore
the	*to look at* theater theory theorem
thec	*case* theca apothecary endothecium
thel	*nipple* thelitis thelerethism epithelium

theo   see **the**

ther   *beast*
                    theriatrics   theriomorphic   therolatry

therap   *treatment*
                    therapy   therapeutic   hydrotherapy

therm   *heat*
                    thermometer   thermostat   diathermy

thes, thet   *to place, to put*
                    thesis   antithesis   synthetic

thet   see **thes**

thi   *sulfur*
                    thiamine   thiazole   thiogenic

thigm   *to touch*
                    thigmotaxis   thigmotropism   thigmocyte

think   *to seem, to appear*
                    think   thought   thanks

thirst   *thirst*
                    thirst   thirsty   athirst

thor   *Thor (god)*
                    thorium   thorite   Thursday

thorac   *chest*
                    thorax   thoracic   thoracoplasty

-thorpe   see **-dorf**

thrall   *slave*
                    thrall   thralldom   enthralled

thrill   *to pierce*
                    thrill   thrilling   nostril

thrix   see **trich**

thromb   *clot*
                    thrombus   thrombosis   thrombokinase

thur   *incense*
                    thurifer   thurible   thurification

thym   *spirit*
                    thymogenic   thymotactic   dysthymia

thym	*thymus (gland)* thymic thymin thymocyte
thyr	*shield, thyroid* thyroid thyreosis thyrosis
tibi	*shinbone, flute* tibia tibiotarsus Tibicen
tic	see **tac**
tim	*to fear* timid intimidate timorous
tim	*honor* timocracy Timothy Timarcha
tin	see **ten**
tinct	see **ting**
ting, tinct	*to dye* tinge tincture taint
-tion	see **-ion**
titan	*Titan* titanic titanium Titanosaurus
tme	see **tom**
toc, tok	*childbirth, child* dystocia epitokous mogitocia
tok	see **toc**
tol	*to raise, to support* extol toll tolerate
tom, tme	*to cut* atom anatomy tmesis
ton, ta, tetan	*stretching, tone* monotone ectasis tetanus
ton	*to thunder* detonate astonish stun
-ton	*town* Washington Boston Carrolton
tons	*to shear, to clip, to cut* tonsure tonsorial tonsor

top	*place* topology topography isotope
tor	*to twist* contortion distort torture
torp	*numb* torpor torpid torpedo
torr	*to burn* torrid torrent thirst
tot	*entirely* total totalitarian totipotential
tourn	*to go around* tournament return attorney
tox	*poison* antitoxin toxemia intoxicate
tra-	see **trans-**
trache	*windpipe* trachea tracheoscopy tracheotomy
trachel	*neck* trachelopexy trachelology trachellate
trachy	*rough* trachyglossate trachyte trachea
tract	*to drag, to draw* tractor extraction tractable
trag	*goat* tragedy tragic tragicomedy
trans-, tra-	*across* transport trans-Atlantic travesty
traumat	*wound, blow* trauma traumatic traumatophobia
treg	*trillion* tregadyne tregerg tregohm
trem, trom	*to shake* tremble tremendous tromometer
tremat	*hole* trematode trematodiasis Trematonotus

trench, trunc	*to cut* trench trenchant truncated
trepan, trypan	*to bore* trepan (n., v.) trepanation trypanosome
tri-	*three* tripod trident trigonometry
trib	*to bestow, to share* contribution tributary retribution
trib	see **trip**
tric	*petty obstacle* extricate intricate intrigue
trich, thrix	*hair* trichina trichinosis trichomycosis
trip, trib	*to rub* entripsis tripsacum nototribe
|**trit**	*to rub* trite contrite detriment
-trix	see **-rix**
troch	*wheel, pulley* trochaic trochophore truck
trochanter	*runner* trochanter trochantin trochanteroplasty
trogl	*hole* troglodyte troglobiont troglotrema
trom	see **trem**
-tron	*suffix from "electron"* cyclotron betatron bevatron
trop	*to turn* tropical heliotrope trophy
troph	*to nourish* trophic atrophy hypertrophy
tru	*faithful* truth trust betrothed

trud, trus	*to thrust* intrude extrude protrusion
trunc	see **trench**
trus	see **trud**
trypan	see **trepan**
tu	*to guard, to look at* tutor tuition intuition
tub	*pipe* tube tuba tubule
tuber	*bump, swelling* tuberous tuberculosis protuberance
-tude	*state, quality, act* servitude latitude magnitude
tum	*to swell* tumor tumescent tumultuous
tunic	*mantle* tunicate tunicin Tunicata
turb	*to agitate* turbulence disturb perturbation
turbin	*to spin* turbine turbinal turbinectomy
turk	*Turkey* turkey Turkish turquoise
turr	*tower* turret turrilite tower
tus	*to pound* contusion obtuse pierce
twi-	*two* twin twilight twine
-ty	*state, quality, that which* liberty beauty property
-ty	*times ten* thirty fifty seventy
tympan	*drum* tympany tympanum tympanectomy

typ	*model, impression*
	typical prototype archetype
typh	*fog, stupor*
	typhus typhoid adenotyphus
typhl	*blind*
	typhlosole typhlostomy typhlectasis
tyr	*cheese*
	tyrosine tyroid tyrogenous
tyrann	*tyrant*
	tyrannical tyrannicide tyrannophobe

U

ubiqu	*everywhere*
	ubiquity ubiquitous ubiquist
ul	*gums*
	ulothrophia uloncus ulocarcinoma
ul	*scar*
	ulosis uloid ulotomy
-ula	see **-ule**
-ule, -ula	*small*
	spherule capsule gastrula
-ulent	*having the quality of*
	corpulent virulent truculent
uln	*elbow*
	ulna ulnar ulnoradial
-ulous	*having the quality of*
	ridiculous fabulous bibulous
ultim	*last*
	ultimate ultimatum penultimate
ultra-, outr-	*beyond*
	ultraviolet ultramodern outrage
-um	*Latin ending*
	modicum pendulum interregnum

umbilic	*navel* umbilicus umbilical umbilectomy
umbr	*shade* umbrella umbrage adumbration
un-	*not* unhappy uncertain unmitigated
unct, oint	*to oil* unction ointment anoint
und	*wave* inundate abundant redundant
-und	see **-cund**
under-	*beneath* undergo undertake understand
ungul	*hoof, claw* ungulate ungulifolia unguligrade
uni-	*one* uniform unison unilateral
-uous	*having the quality of* impetuous tortuous sumptuous
ur	*tail* anurous urochord squirrel
ur, uret	*urine* urology urogenital urethra
uran	*sky, heavens* Uranus uranium uranography
urb	*city* urban urbane suburban
-ure	*state, quality, act* departure rupture primogeniture
-ure	*that which* creature furniture debenture
uret	see **ur**
urg	see **erg**
urin	*urine* urinalysis urinology uriniferous

urs	*bear (animal)*
	ursine *Ursa Major* ursiform
-us	*Latin ending*
	focus gladiolus impetus
us, ut	*to use*
	abuse utensil utility
ut	*out*
	utter (adj.) utter (v.) utmost
ut	see **us**
uter	*uterus, womb*
	uterine uterocele uterolith
utop	*no-place*
	Utopia utopian utopographer
utricul	*small bag*
	utricle utricular Utricularia
uvul	*little grape*
	uvula uvulitis uvulectomy
uxor	*wife*
	uxorial uxorious uxoricide

V

vac	*empty*
	vacant evacuate vacation
vacc	*cow*
	vaccine vaccinate vaccination
vad, vas	*to go*
	invade evade pervasive
vag	*to wander*
	vagrant vagabond extravagant
vagin	*sheath*
	vagina vaginal vanilla
val	*to be strong*
	valid value equivalent

val	*valley* vale valley avalanche
valv	*folding door* valve bivalve valvular
van	*empty* vanish evanescent vanity
vanad	*Vanadis (goddess), vanadium* vanadic vanadiferous vanadite
vap	*steam* vapor evaporate vapid
var	*diverse* various variety variegate
varic	*(dilated) vein* varicose varicotomy varicoid
variol	*pox* variola variolate variolite
vas	*vessel* vascular vasectomy vasoconstrictor
vas	see **vad**
vect	see **veh**
veg	*to enliven* vegetation vegetate vegetable
veh, vect	*to carry* vehicle vehement convection
vel	*veil, covering* velum velar revelation
veloc	*fast* velocity velocipede velocimeter
ven	*to come* convention revenue intervene
ven	*vein* venesection venous venation
vend	*to sell* vend vendor venal

venen *poison*
veneniferous   venom   veneno-salivary

vener *sexual*
venereal   venery   venerologist

vent *wind*
ventilator   ventilation   ventometer

ventr *stomach*
ventral   ventriloquist   ventrotomy

ver *true*
verify   verdict   veracious

verb *word*
verbal   adverb   verbiage

verg *to lean*
verge   converge   divergent

verm *worm*
vermin   vermiform   vermicelli

verruc *wart*
verruca   verrucous   verruciform

vers see **vert**

vert, vers *to turn*
revert   advertise   versatile

vertebr *joint, vertebra*
vertebra   vertebrectomy   invertebrate

vesic *bladder, blister*
vesicle   vesicant   vesicular

vest *to dress*
vest   vestment   investment

vestig *footprint*
vestige   vestigial   investigate

vet *old*
veteran   inveterate   veterinary

via *way, road*
via   viaduct   trivial

vic *substitute*
vicarious   vicar   vice-president

-vich	*son of* Ivanovich Petrovich Grigorevich
vicin	*neighbor* vicinity vicinal vicinage
vict	see **vinc**
vid, vis	*to see* provide television invisible
vig	*lively* vigilant vigil vigorous
vil	*cheap* vile vilify vilification
vill	*country dwelling* village villa villain
vill	*velvet, shaggy* villus villiform velvet
-ville	*city, town* Abbeville Joinville Placerville
vin	*wine* vintage vinegar viniculture
vinc, vict	*to conquer* convince invincible victorious
vinc, vict	*conqueror* Vincent Victor Victoria
violac	*violet* violaceous violescent Violaceae
vir	*man* virile triumvirate virtue
vir	*poison, virus* virus virulent virology
virid	*green* viridescent viridity viridigenous
vis	see **vid**
visc	*sticky* viscous viscosity viscid

viscer	*belly, internal organs* visceral visceromotor viscerotome
vit	*grapevine* viticulture viticetum vitiferous
vita	*life* vital vitamins revitalize
vitell	*yolk* vitellus vitelline vitellaria
vitr	*glass* vitreous vitrify vitriol
viv	*to live* revive vivid vivisection
voc, voke	*voice, to call* vocal vociferous revoke
vol	*to will* volunteer volition benevolent
volu	see **volv**
volv, volu	*to roll* revolve evolution volume
vomer	*plowshare* vomer vomerine vomeronasal
vor	*to eat* voracious carnivore omnivorous
vot	*to vow* vote votive devotion
vulcan	*Vulcan (god)* vulcanize volcano volcanology
vulg	*common* vulgar divulge Vulgate
vuln	*wound* vulnerable invulnerable vulture
vulp	*fox* vulpine vulpecide Vulpes
vuls	*to tug* convulse convulsion revulsion

W

wak	*to be awake* awaken watch wait
wal	*foreign, Celtic* walnut Wales Walloon
war	*aware* wary unaware beware
ward	*to protect* warden wardrobe reward
-ward	*toward* upward windward backward
warf	*to turn* wharf whirl whorl
warn	*to protect* warning warrant warranty
weiss	*white* edelweiss Weisshorn bismuth
wer	*to wear* wearer wore worn
whisk	*to flick* whisk whiskers whisk-broom
-wich, -wick	*town* Norwich Sandwich Warwick
-wick	see **-wich**
wif	*female* wife wifely woman
wis	see **wit**
-wise	*in the manner of* clockwise likewise lengthwise
wit, wis	*to know* witty witness wisdom
with-	*against* withstand withdraw withhold

worth   *value*
worthy   worship   stalwart

wring   *to twist*
wring   wrong   wrench

writh   *to twist*
writhe   wrath   wreath

wroht   *to work*
wrought   cartwright   playwright

X

xanth   *yellow*
xanthous   xanthophyll   xanthoderma

xen   *foreign, strange*
xenophobia   xenolith   xenon

xer   *dry*
xerophilous   xerophagous   xerography

xiph   *sword*
xiphoid   xiphophyllous   xiphocostal

xyl   *wood*
xylophone   xyloma   xylography

Y

-y   *having the quality of*
gloomy   dirty   hasty

-y, -ie   *small*
doggy   kitty   Maggie

-y   *something done*
injury   augury   colloquy

-y   *state, quality, act*
melancholy   history   astronomy

-yer	see **-er**
yl	see **hyl**
ytterb	*Ytterby (in Sweden)* ytterbium yttrium terbium

Z

zeal	*fervor* zealot zealous jealous
zephyr	*westwind* zephyr zephyrean Zephyranthes
zeug	see **zyg**
zinc	*zinc* zincite zinciferous zincography
zircon	*zircon* zirconium zirconate zirconic
zo	*animal* zoology protozoon spermatozoon
-zoic	*animal, life* cytozoic Cenozoic Mesozoic
zon	*belt* zone zonal zonoplacental
zyg, zeug	*yoke, paired* zygote heterozygous zygodactyl
zym	*ferment* enzyme zymology zymurgy

SECTION 2

English-to-Roots

A

to abandon	*lip*
abdomen	*abdomin*
able to (be)	*-able*
able to be	*-ible*
able to (be)	*-ile*
to be able	*mag*
to be able	*pot, poss*
above	*hyper-*
above	*over-*
above	*super-, supra-, sur-*
absence	*lev*
abundance	*copi*
acetone	*ket*
acid	*acid*
acid	*oxy*
acorn	*balan*
across	*trans-, tra-*
act	*-acy, -cy*
act	*-age*
act	*-ance*

act	-ancy
act	-asia, -asis
act	-asm
to act	-ate
act	-ence
act	-ency
act	-ery, -ry
act	-esis
act	-ety
act of	-ice
act	-ion, -tion
act	-ism
act	-ity
to act	-ize, -ise
act	-ment
act	-osis, -sis
act	-tude
act	-ure
act	-y
to adjust	apt, ept
to advise	moni
to advise	suad, suas
from afar	tele-
after	post-
after	poster-
again	ana-
again	palin, pali
again	re-
against	ad-
against	anti-, ant-
against	contra-, counter-

against	*for-*
against	*ob-, oc-, of-, op-*
against	*with-*
age	*ev*
to agitate	*turb*
to agree	*pact*
agreeable	*suav*
air	*aer*
air	*aur*
air	*loft*
all	*omni-*
all	*pan-, panto-*
to allow	*lack*
to allow	*lax*
to allow	*leas, laiss*
to allow	*lef*
to allow	*lev*
almond	*amygdal*
almost	*pen*
alone	*erem*
alone	*mono-*
alone	*sol*
amber	*electr*
America	*americ*
amnion	*amni*
amoeba	*amoeb*
ancient	*pale, palai*
angel	*angel*
angle	*angul, angl*
angle	*gon*
animal	*zo*

animal	*-zoic*
ankle	*tal*
ankle-bone	*astragal*
to announce	*nunc, nounce*
to anoint	*unct, oint*
anointed	*christ*
ant	*formic*
ant	*myrmec*
antimony	*stib*
anus	*an*
anus	*proct*
anvil	*incud*
apart	*se-*
ape	*pithec*
Aphrodite	*aphrodis*
to appear	*par*
to appear	*phan, phen*
to appear	*think*
appetite	*orex*
to applaud	*plaud*
apple	*mel*
apple	*pom*
arc	*arc*
arch	*fornic*
area	*chor*
arm	*brac*
arm	*brachi*
arms	*arm*
arms	*opl*
army	*strat*
around	*ambi-, amphi-*

around	*circum-*
around	*peri-*
to go around	*tourn*
arrangement	*tax, tact*
arsenic	*arsen*
art	*art*
art	*techn*
artery	*arter*
ash	*ciner*
to be ashamed	*pud*
to ask	*bid, bead*
to ask	*quest, quir, quis*
to ask	*rog*
ass	*asin*
to assess	*cens*
at	*a-*
Athena	*athen*
Atlas	*atlant*
atrium	*atri*
to attend to	*med*
awake	*vig*
to be awake	*wak*
aware	*war*
away	*ab-*
away	*apo-, ap-*
away	*cata-, cath-, cat-*
away	*de-*
away	*dis-, di-, dif-*
away	*e-, ex-*
away	*ec-*
away	*for-*

away	*se-*
axis	*ax, axon*
axis	*pol*

B

to babble	*lal*
Bacchus	*bacch*
bacillus	*bacill*
back	*ana-*
back	*back*
back (of body)	*dors*
back (of body)	*noto-*
back	*opistho-*
back	*palin, pali*
back	*re-*
back (of body)	*terg*
backwards	*retro-*
spherical bacterium	*cocc*
bad	*cac*
bad	*dys-*
bad	*mal*
bad	*mis-*
badly	*dys-*
badly	*mal*
badly	*mis-*
bag	*asc*
bag	*bel*
bag	*bulg*
bag	*burs*

bag	*foll*
bag	*sac*
small bag	*utricul*
to bake	*bak*
balance	*liber, libr*
ball	*ball*
ball of yarn	*glom*
ball	*pil*
ball	*spher*
band	*fasci*
band	*sphincter*
to banish	*ban*
(river-) bank	*rip, riv*
bare	*gym*
bare	*nud*
bark	*cortic*
to base	*fund, found*
basin	*pelv*
basin	*pyel*
battle	*-machy*
to be	*ess, ent*
beak	*rostr*
bear (animal)	*arct*
to bear	*ber*
to bear	*gest, ger*
to bear	*lat*
to bear	*ois, es*
to bear	*par, part*
to bear	*phor, pher*
to bear	*port*
bear (animal)	*urs*

to bear	*veh, vect*
beard	*pogon*
bearing	*-ferous*
beast	*ther*
beautiful	*bell*
beautiful	*calli*
beauty	*cosmet*
beauty	*pulchr*
becoming (proper)	*dec*
becoming	*-escent*
bed	*lit*
bedbug	*cimic*
bee	*api*
before	*ante-*
before	*anter-*
before	*ere*
before	*fore-*
before	*pre-, prae-*
before	*pro-*
to beget	*kin*
behind	*aft*
behind	*poster-*
being	*ont*
to believe	*cred*
bell	*calyc*
bell	*campan*
bellows	*foll*
bellows	*phys*
belly	*coeli*
belly	*viscer*
below	*hypo-, hyp-*

below	*infra-*
below	*neth*
below	*sub-, suc-, suf-, sug-, sup-, sur-*
below	*under-*
belt	*cinct*
belt	*zon*
bench	*bank*
to bend	*bow*
bend	*croc*
to bend	*flect, flex*
beneath	*hypo-, hyp-*
beneath	*infra-*
beneath	*neth*
beneath	*sub-, suc-, suf-, sug-, sup-, sur-*
beneath	*under-*
Bengal (India)	*bengal*
berry	*bacc*
berry	*cocc*
beside	*juxta-*
beside	*para-, par-*
best	*optim*
to bestow	*trib*
better	*melior*
between	*dia-, di-*
between	*enter-, entre-*
between	*inter-*
beyond	*meta-, met-*
beyond	*preter-*
beyond	*ultra-, outr-*
big	*macro-*
big	*magn-*

big	*maha-*
big	*mega-, megal-, meg-*
bigger	*major*
biggest	*maxim*
bile	*bil*
bile	*chol*
to bind	*bind*
to bind	*cinct*
to bind	*lig*
to bind	*sphing, sphinx*
to bind	*string, strict*
bird	*avi*
bird	*ornith*
birth	*gen*
birth	*toc, tok*
to bite	*mors, mord*
bitter	*alum*
bitter	*amar*
bitter	*picr*
black	*atr*
black	*melan*
black	*nigr*
bladder	*cyst*
bladder	*phys*
bladder	*vesic*
blame	*culp*
blind	*caec, cec*
blind	*typhl*
blister	*vesic*
blood	*bled, blod*
blood	*hem, haem, em*

blood	*sanguin*
blood vessel	*angi*
to blow	*blaw*
to blow	*fla*
a blow	*traumat*
blue	*caes, ces*
blue	*cerule*
blue	*cyan*
board	*barr*
board	*bord*
board	*tabl*
boat	*cymb*
boat	*scaph*
body	*corp*
body	*som, somat*
to boil	*ferv*
bond	*clam*
bond	*copul*
bond	*des, dem*
bone	*oss*
bone	*oste*
book	*bibli*
book	*libr*
booty	*pred*
booty	*rob, rev*
to bore (through)	*trepan, trypan*
to be born	*nat, nasc*
to be born	*ori, ort*
both	*ambi-, amphi-*
bottom	*basi*
bottom	*byss, byth*

bottom	*edaph*
bottom	*grund*
to bound	*hor*
boundary	*mark*
bow	*arc*
bowl	*amni*
bowl	*cymb*
box	*caps*
brain	*cerebr*
brain	*encephal*
brain	*phren*
branch	*ram*
bread	*pan*
to break	*brek*
to break	*clas*
to break	*frag, fract*
to break	*rupt*
breast	*brest*
breast	*mamm*
breast	*mast*
breast	*maz*
breast	*stern*
breast	*steth*
breath	*anim*
breath	*atm*
breath	*spir*
to breathe	*pneumon, pneum, pne*
breathless	*asthm*
breeze	*aur*
breeze	*flabell*
bridge	*-bridge, -bruck*

bridge	*pont*
bright	*agla*
bright	*bert*
bristle	*chaet, chet*
to bristle	*horr*
bristle	*set*
broad	*brad*
broad	*platy-*
bronze	*aene*
bronze	*chalc*
brother	*adelph*
brother	*frater*
brown	*aeth*
brown	*brun*
bubble	*bull*
to bubble	*ferv*
buckle	*fibul*
bud	*blast*
bud	*gemm*
bud	*germ*
to build	*struct*
builder	*tect*
bull	*taur*
bump	*tuber*
burden	*mol*
to burn	*arid*
to burn	*burn, bran*
to burn	*caust, caut*
to burn	*ether*
to burn	*flagr*
to burn	*torr*

burnt	*aeth*
to burn up	*combur*
to burst	*-rrhage, -rrhex*
bush	*shrub*
butter	*butyr*
butterfly	*papilion*
buttocks	*glute*
buttocks	*pyg*
to buy	*cheap*
to buy	*empt*

C

(Julius) Caesar	*caesar*
to call	*voc, voke*
callus	*por*
camp	*-caster, -cester*
canal	*canal*
cancer	*cancer, chancr*
cancer	*carcin*
cape	*cap*
carbuncle	*anthrac*
card	*cart*
care	*cur*
carpet	*tapet*
to carry	*ber*
to carry	*fer*
to carry	*gest, ger*
to carry	*lat*
to carry	*ois, es*
to carry	*phor, pher*

to carry	*port*
to carry	*veh, vect*
cartilage	*chondr*
to carve	*glyph*
to carve	*sculp*
case	*thec*
cat	*ailur, aelur*
cat	*cat*
cat	*fel*
head of cattle	*capit*
cattle	*fe*
cattle	*pecu*
cause	*etio-*
cause	*gen*
causing	*-ferous*
cave	*spel*
cavern	*antr*
to cease	*paus*
cell	*cell*
cell	*cyt*
Celtic	*wal*
center	*centr*
cerebrum	*cerebr*
Ceres	*cere*
chain	*caten*
chalk	*cret*
chamber	*camer*
(inner) chamber	*thalam*
chance	*sort*
change	*amoeb*
change	*meta-, met-*

to change	*mut*
channel	*solen*
channel	*stria*
character	*eth*
charcoal	*carbo*
charge	*crimin*
cheap	*vil*
cheek	*bucc*
cheese	*case*
cheese	*tyr*
chemical element	*-ium*
chest	*pector*
chest	*stern*
chest	*steth*
chest	*thorac*
chicken	*poul*
(unborn) child	*fet*
child	*ped*
child	*pup*
child	*toc, tok*
childbirth	*toc, tok*
children	*prol*
chin	*ment*
China	*sin*
chi-shaped (X)	*chias*
to choose	*leg, lig, lect*
to choose	*opt*
to chop	*hatch*
Christ	*christ*
church	*eccles*
cilium	*blephar*

circle	*cycl*
circle	*gyr*
circle	*orb*
citizen	*civ*
citrus	*citr*
city	*-abad*
city	*-grad, gorod*
city	*poli, polit*
city	*-polis*
city	*urb*
city	*-ville*
clavicle	*clavic*
clavicle	*cleid, cleis*
claw	*chel*
claw	*onych*
claw	*ungul*
clean	*clean*
clean	*mund*
clean	*pur*
to clean	*purg*
clear	*clar*
clearing	*-ley*
to climb	*scend, scens, scent*
to clip	*tons*
cloak	*palli*
to close	*clud, clus, claus, close*
clot	*thromb*
cloth	*cloth*
small cloth	*pan*
clothes	*vest*
clothing	*dysi*

club	*clav*
club	*coryn*
coal	*anthrac*
coal	*carbo*
coast	*cost*
cobalt	*cobalt*
cock	*alector, alectry*
coil	*spir*
cold	*col, chil*
cold	*cry, kry*
cold	*crym*
cold	*frig*
cold	*psychr*
color	*chrom, chro*
color	*color*
column	*styl*
comb	*cten*
comb	*pectin*
to come	*come*
to come	*ven*
to command	*mand*
common	*cen, coen*
common	*vulg*
companion	*comit*
companion	*soci*
to complain	*quer*
completion	*tele, teli, telo*
condition	*-ia*
condition	*-iasis*
condition	*-osis, -sis*
cone	*con*

to conquer	*vinc, vict*
conqueror	*vinc, vict*
container	*caps*
contest	*athl*
convulsion	*spasm*
to cook	*coct*
copper	*aene*
copper	*chalc*
copper	*cupr*
to copy	*mim*
coral	*corall*
corner	*gon*
correct	*orth-*
to correct	*put*
correct	*rect*
to count	*tell, tal*
countless	*myria-*
country	*rus, rur*
country	*-stan*
country dwelling	*vill*
county	*shire*
course	*drom*
to cover	*cover*
to cover	*teg, tect*
covered	*calypt*
(hard) covering	*crust*
covering	*steg*
covering	*vel*
cow	*bou, bov*
cow	*vacc*
crab	*cancer, chancr*

crab	*carcin*
to crack	*crak*
to crack	*crepit*
to crackle	*crepit*
craft	*art*
craft	*techn*
crane (bird)	*geran*
craving	*mania*
to creep	*rept*
to creep	*snak*
crime	*crimin*
to croak	*crek*
crooked	*ankyl, ancyl*
crooked	*kyph*
crooked	*prav*
crooked	*scoli*
cross	*cruc*
crossbar	*cancel*
crown	*coron*
crude	*rud*
to cry	*plor*
crystal	*cryst*
cuckoo	*coccyg*
cup	*calyc*
cup	*cotyl*
cup	*cyath*
cup	*scyph*
curl	*cirr, cirrh*
curv	*sinus, sinu*
curved	*campt*
curved	*campyl*

curved	*curv*
curved	*falc*
cushion	*pulvin*
custom	*eth*
custom	*mor*
to cut	*-cide, cis*
to cut	*cop*
to cut	*coup*
to cut	*sect, sec*
to cut	*shear, shor*
to cut	*tail*
to cut	*tom, tme*
to cut	*tons*
to cut	*trench, trunc*
Cyprus	*cypr*

D

to damage	*lid, lis*
to dance	*chor*
to dance	*orch*
dark	*amaur*
dark	*fusc*
dark	*maur*
darkness	*scot*
daughter of	*-ovna*
dawn	*eo-*
day	*day*
day	*dia*
day	*hemer*
day	*journ*

dead	*necr, nec*
dear	*car*
dear	*lef*
death	*bane*
death	*leth*
death	*mort*
death	*necr, nec*
death	*thanat, than*
decay	*cari*
to deceive	*fall, fals*
to declare	*say*
to decorate	*orn*
deep	*bath*
deer	*elaph*
to define	*hor*
delta-shaped ($\triangle$)	*delt*
demon	*demon*
dense	*das*
to deny	*neg*
depth	*byss, byth*
descendant of	*-ek, -ik*
descendant of	*-ez*
to desire	*av*
to desire	*cup*
to desire	*desider*
to destroy	*del*
devil	*cobalt*
devil	*diabol*
devil	*nickel*
to devour	*vor*
to die	*star*

to dig	*grav*
to digest	*pept, peps*
dinner	*deipn*
to dip	*bapt*
to dip	*merg, mers*
direction whence	*-erly*
disease	*morb*
disease	*nos*
disease	*path*
dish	*patell*
disk	*disc*
disturb	*stir*
ditch	*foss*
diverse	*var*
to divide	*shear, shor*
divination	*-mancy*
to do	*ag, ig, act*
to do	*-ate*
to do	*don*
to do	*dra*
to do	*fac, fic, fect, -fy*
to do	*-ize, -ise*
to do	*pract, prax*
dog	*can, cyn*
doll	*cor*
doll	*pup*
dolphin	*delph*
something done	*-em*
something done	*-eme*
something done	*-ma*
something done	*-men*

something done	*-y*
door	*for*
door	*osti*
(folding) door	*valv*
doorway	*jan*
doorway	*port*
double	*diplo-*
dough	*past*
dove	*columb*
down	*cata-, cath-, cat-*
down	*de-*
to drag	*tract*
to draw	*drag*
to draw	*tract*
dress	*vest*
to drink	*bib*
to drink	*drink*
to drink	*pot, pos*
to drip	*drip*
dripping	*stalagm, stalact*
to drive	*ag, ig, act*
to drive	*drif*
a drop	*gutt*
a drop	*stil*
drug	*pharmac*
drum	*tympan*
dry	*arid*
dry	*dryg*
dry	*scel*
dry	*sicc, sec*
dry	*xer*

dull	*ambly*
dull	*hebet*
struck dumb	*stup*
dung	*copr*
dung	*guan*
dung	*scat, skat*
dung	*sterc*
dust	*coni, koni*
dust	*pulver*
dwarf	*nan*
to dye	*ting, tinct*

E

eagle	*aquil*
ear	*aur*
ear	*ot*
eardrum	*myring*
early	*eo-*
to earn	*mer*
earth	*chamae*
earth	*chthon*
earth	*ge*
earth	*tellur*
earth	*terr*
ease	*oti*
east	*anatol*
east	*euro-*
east	*orient*
to eat	*phag*
to eat	*vor*

egg	*oö-*
egg	*ov*
eight	*octo-, oct-*
elbow	*uln*
electric	*electr*
suffix from "electron"	*-tron*
chemical element	*-ium*
empty	*cen*
empty	*jejun*
empty	*vac*
empty	*van*
enclosure	*cohort*
enclosure	*geard*
enclosure	*phragm, phrax*
enclosure	*sty*
end	*fin*
end	*tele, teli, telo*
end	*termin, term*
English	*angl*
full enjoyment	*fruct*
to enliven	*veg*
enough	*sat*
to entice	*lic*
entirely	*tot*
to entrust	*mand*
equal	*equ*
equal	*iso-*
equal	*par*
to establish	*fund, found*
evening	*hesper*
everywhere	*ubiqu*

to examine	*skep*
to excavate	*dig*
to excite	*hormon*
to extend	*strec*
extremity	*acro*
extremity	*apic*
eye	*ocul*
eye	*omma, ommat*
eye	*op*
eye	*ophthalm*
eyelash	*cili*
eyelid	*blephar*
eyelid	*cili*
(edge of) eyelid	*tars*

F

face	*fac*
face	*prosop*
faith	*fid*
faithful	*tru*
to fall	*cad, cid, cas*
to fall	*pto*
falling	*caduc*
falling	*occident*
false	*pseud*
false	*spuri*
fame	*ro*
farmer	*bor*
farmer	*georg*
to fashion	*fig*

fast	*celer*
fast	*tach*
fast	*veloc*
to fasten	*fix*
to fasten	*pact*
to fasten	*pec, pex, pag*
fasting	*jejun*
fat	*adip*
fat	*lip, lipo-*
fat	*seb*
fat	*steat, stear*
father	*pap, pop*
father	*pater*
fault	*culp*
fault	*mend*
favor	*charis*
to fear	*phob*
to fear	*tim*
feast	*fest*
feather	*pinn, pinnat, penn*
feather	*plum*
feather	*pter*
feathered	*fledge*
to feed	*fed*
to feed	*past*
to feel	*sens, sent*
feeler	*palp*
feeling	*esthet, esthes*
feeling	*path*
female	*femin*
female	*wif*

feminine	*-a*
feminine	*-ess*
feminine	*-rix, -trix*
fence	*phragm, phrax*
to ferment	*brew*
ferment	*zym*
fern	*pterid*
fervor	*zeal*
fever	*febr*
fever	*pyret*
few	*oligo-*
few	*pauci-*
fiber	*fibr*
fiber	*in*
field	*agr*
field	*camp*
to fight	*-machy*
to fight	*milit*
to fight	*pugn*
figure	*schemat*
to filter	*col*
filthy	*ful*
fin	*branchi*
to find	*heur*
finger	*dactyl*
finger	*digit*
fire	*ign*
fire	*pyr*
first	*arch*
first	*prim, prin*
first	*proto-*

fish	*ichthy*
fish	*pisc*
to fit	*apt, ept*
fitting	*met*
five	*penta-*
five	*quinqu-, quint-*
flame	*flam*
flame	*phlegm*
flame	*phlog*
flank	*lapar*
flask	*ampull*
flat	*plac*
flat	*plan*
flat	*platy-*
flat cake	*placent*
flat ground	*sol*
flax	*byss*
flax	*lin*
to flee	*fug*
Flemish	*flem, flam*
flesh	*carn*
flesh	*creat-, cre-, kre-*
flesh	*sarc*
to flick	*whisk*
flint	*silic*
to float	*flot*
flock	*greg*
flour	*aleur*
flour	*far*
to flow	*flu, flux*
to flow	*-rrhage, -rrhex*

to flow	*-rrhea*
flower	*anth*
flower	*flor*
flower (name)	*-ia*
to fluctuate	*oscill*
fluid	*chyl*
fluid	*chym*
fluid	*liqu*
flute	*aul*
flute	*tibi*
a fly	*musc*
foam	*aphr*
focus	*foc*
fog	*typh*
-fold	*-fold*
-fold	*-ple*
to fold	*plex, plic, ply*
to follow	*sequ, sec*
food	*met*
food	*sit, siti*
foolish	*fatu*
foot	*fot, fet*
foot	*ped*
foot	*pod, pus*
footprint	*vestig*
for	*pro-*
(river) ford	*-ford*
forehead	*front*
foreign	*barbar*
foreign	*wal*
foreign	*xen*

forest	*silv, sylv*
to forget	*leth*
to forget	*obliv*
fork	*furc*
form	*eido-*
form	*form*
form	*morph*
to form	*plas*
form	*schemat*
form	*shape*
fort	*-burg, -burgh*
fort	*-bury, -borough*
fort	*-caster, -cester*
forward	*pro-*
forward	*pros-*
foul matter	*pur, pus*
four	*quadr-, quart*
four	*tetra*
fox	*vulp*
French	*franc*
French	*gall*
free	*eleuther*
free	*franc*
free	*grat*
free	*liber*
to free	*lys, lyt*
to free	*solv, solu*
freeman	*carl*
to frighten	*terr*
fringe	*fimbr*
frog	*ran*

from	*ab-*
from	*apo-, ap-*
from	*cata-, cath-, cat-*
from	*de-*
from	*dis-, di-, dif-*
from	*e-, ex-*
from	*ec-*
front	*anter-*
front	*pros-*
frost	*crym*
frost	*gel*
fruit	*carp*
fruit	*fruct*
fruit	*pom*
fruit-stone	*pyren*
full	*plen, plet, -ply*
full	*pleth*
fungus	*agaric*
fungus	*myc*
funnel	*choan*
furrow	*sulc*

G

gall	*bil*
gall	*chol*
gap	*hiat*
garden	*cohort*
garden	*geard*
gas	*man*
gate	*port*

gate	*pyl*
to gather	*leg, lig, lect*
German	*german*
to get	*get*
giant	*gigant*
gift	*dor*
gift	*mun*
gill	*branchi*
girdle	*cest*
girdle	*cinct*
girdle	*zon*
to give	*don, dat*
to give	*dos, dot*
to give	*gif*
gland	*aden*
gland	*balan*
glass	*hyal*
glass	*vitr*
to glide	*slip*
glowing	*cand*
glue	*coll*
glue	*gli*
glue	*glutin*
to gnaw	*rode, ros*
to go	*bas, bat, bet*
to go	*cede, ceed, cess*
to go	*fare*
to go	*it*
to go	*vad, vas*
to go up	*sti*
goat	*aeg*

goat	*capr*
goat	*trag*
God	*dei, div*
God	*god*
God	*the, theo*
God's gracious gift	*joan, john*
gold	*aur*
gold	*chrys*
good	*agath*
good	*bene-*
good	*bon*
good	*eu-*
good	*prob*
goose	*anser*
goose	*chen*
goose	*gos*
grain	*chondr*
grain	*far*
grain	*gran*
grain	*sit, siti*
grainy	*granat*
grandson of	*o'*
grape	*acin*
little grape	*uvul*
bunch of grapes	*staphyl*
grapevine	*vit*
grass	*gramin*
grass	*herb*
gratitude	*charis*
gray	*cani*
gray	*poli*

gray-green	*glauc*
to graze	*bosc, bot*
great	*grand*
great	*macro-*
great	*magn-*
great	*maha-*
great	*mega-, megal-, meg-*
greater	*magister*
greater	*major*
greatest	*maxim*
Greek ending	*-on*
Greek plural ending	*-a*
green	*chlor*
green	*pras*
green	*virid*
gridiron	*rost*
grief	*dol*
to grieve	*murn*
to grind	*mael*
to grind (grain)	*mol*
gristle	*cartilag*
groin	*ile*
groin	*ili*
ground	*edaph*
ground	*hum*
ground	*ped*
group	*-ad*
group	*-ida*
group	*-ome*
to grow	*cresc, crease, cret, cru*

to grow	*grow*
growth	*-oma*
growth	*phym*
guard	*custod*
guard	*phylac*
to guard	*tu*
to guide	*tech*
gums	*gingiv*
gums	*ul*

H

hailstone	*chalaz*
hair	*capill*
hair	*com*
hair	*crin*
hair	*pil*
hair	*trich, thrix*
half	*demi-*
half	*hemi-*
half	*med*
half	*mezz*
half	*semi-*
hammer	*malle*
hand	*chir, cheir*
hand	*manu*
handle	*ans*
to hang	*aort*
to hang	*hang*
to hang	*pend, pens*
to hang over	*min*

to happen	*cad, cid, cas*
happy	*felic*
harbor	*port*
hard	*dur*
hard	*hard, -ard*
hard	*scirrh*
hard	*scler*
harmony	*cosm*
harmony	*cosmet*
harrow	*hears*
hatchet	*pelecy*
to hate	*mis-*
to hate	*odi*
to have	*hab*
to have	*hav*
to have	*own*
head	*capit*
head	*cephal*
back of head	*occip*
head	*poll*
headband	*mitr*
healing	*iatr*
health	*hygi*
health	*salut*
healthy	*hal*
healthy	*hol*
healthy	*san*
to be healthy	*val*
heap	*cumul*
heap	*mol*
to hear	*acou, acu*

to hear	*audi*
to hear	*her*
heart	*card*
heart	*cord*
heart	*heart*
heat	*therm*
heaven	*cel*
heavenly	*-lani*
heavens	*uran*
heavy	*grav*
to heed	*reck*
heel	*calc*
heir	*her, hered*
Hermes	*herm*
hernia	*-cele*
hidden	*calypt*
hidden	*crypt, krypt*
to lie hidden	*lanthan, lat*
to hide	*cell*
to hide	*cond*
to hide	*cover*
to hide	*hel*
high	*acro*
high	*alt*
high	*haut*
high	*hyps*
highest point	*summ*
hill	*mount, mont*
hip	*cox*
hip	*ischi*

hip	*sciat*
to hold	*hald*
to hold	*hec, hex, ech*
to hold	*ten, tin, tain*
hole	*hol*
hole	*tremat*
hollow	*can*
hollow	*cav*
hollow	*coel, cel*
hollow	*colp*
hollow	*lacun*
hollow	*scaph*
hollow	*sinus, sinu*
holy	*hagi*
holy	*hal*
holy	*pi*
holy	*sacr*
holy	*san, sant*
holy	*sanct*
home	*dom*
home	*eco-, oec*
home	*ham, -heim, home*
honey	*mell*
honeycomb	*fav*
honor	*tim*
honored	*sebast*
hoof	*chel*
hoof	*ungul*
hook	*croc*
hook	*onc*
to hope	*sper*

horn	*corn*
horn	*kerat, cerat*
horse	*caval*
horse	*equ*
horse	*hipp*
hot	*cal*
hour	*hor*
house	*cas*
house	*hus, hous*
human being	*anthrop*
human being	*homo*
human being	*man*
humpbacked	*kyph*
hundred	*cent*
hundred	*hecto-, hecato-*
husband	*marit*

I

I	*ego*
ice	*glac*
idea	*ideo-*
ileum	*ile*
ilium	*ili*
image	*icon*
image	*idol*
to imitate	*mim*
to impel	*cit*
impression	*typ*
in	*a-*

in	*en-, em-*
in	*in-, im-, il-, ir-*
incense	*thur*
to increase	*aug*
to increase	*aux*
Indian	*ind*
inferior	*-aster*
inflammation	*-itis*
information about	*-ana*
-ing	*-ant*
-ing	*-end, -and*
-ing	*-ent*
-ing	*-ion, -tion*
to inhabit	*col, cult*
to injure	*noc, nox*
insanity	*mania*
insect	*entom*
inside	*endo-*
inside	*int-*
inside	*intro-, intra-*
instep	*tars*
instrument	*organ*
intensive	*be-*
intensive	*com-, co-, col-, con-, cor-*
intensive	*en-, em-*
intensive	*per-, pel-*
internal organs	*viscer*
to interpret	*red*
large intestine	*col*
intestine	*enter*
into	*en-, em-*

into	*in-, im-, il-, ir-*
iris (of eye)	*irid*
Irish	*hibern*
iron	*ferr*
iron	*sider*
island	*insul*
island	*nes*
Italian	*ital*
itch	*psor*
ivory	*eburn*

J

jackass	*asin*
jaw	*gnath*
lower jaw	*mandib*
jaw	*maxill*
Jewish	*jud*
to join	*junct, jug, join*
joined	*zyg, zeug*
joint	*arthr, art*
joint	*vertebr*
joke	*joc*
Jove (Jupiter)	*jov*
to judge	*cri*
to judge	*dem*
judge	*jud*
judgment	*sap*
juice	*chyl*
juice	*chym*
to jump	*sal, sil, sult*

K

Kadmos (Greek hero)	*cadm*
kernel	*nucle*
key	*clav*
key	*cleid, cleis*
kidney	*nephr*
kidney	*ren*
to kill	*-cide, cis*
kind	*gen*
what kind	*qual*
king	*basil*
king	*reg*
knee	*gen, gon*
knife	*cutl*
knot	*gangli*
to knot	*nect*
knot	*nod*
to know (how)	*can, con, ken*
to know	*cogn*
to know	*gnos, gnom*
to know	*know*
to know	*no*
to know	*sci*
to know	*wit, wis*
knuckle	*condyl*

L

L	*lambd*
to lack	*lip*

to lack	*-penia*
ladder	*climac*
ladder	*scala*
lady	*dam*
lambda (λ, Λ)	*lambd*
lame	*claud*
to lament	*plain*
language	*gloss, glot*
language	*lingu*
larger	*major*
largest	*maxim*
larva	*larv*
last	*eschat*
last	*fin*
last	*ultim*
lasting	*dur*
late	*opsi-*
late	*tard*
Latin ending	*-a*
Latin ending	*-um*
Latin ending	*-us*
Latin plural ending	*-a*
Latin plural ending	*-ae*
Latin plural ending	*-i*
lattice	*cancel*
to laugh	*gel, gelot*
to laugh	*rid, ris*
law	*leg*
law	*nom*
to lay	*leg*
layer	*lamin, lamell*

to lead	*duc*
to lead	*led*
to lead	*men*
lead (metal)	*molybd*
lead (metal)	*plumb*
leader	*agog*
leaf	*foli*
leaf	*lamin, lamell*
leaf	*petal*
leaf	*phyll*
to lean	*clin, climat*
to lean	*verg*
to leap	*leap*
to leap	*sal, sil, sult*
to learn	*math*
least	*minim*
leather	*cor*
to leave	*linqu, lict*
to leave	*lip*
left hand	*levo-, laevo-*
left hand	*sinistr*
leg	*crur*
leg	*scel*
leisure	*oti*
leisure	*schol*
lens	*phac, phak*
lentil	*lent*
lentil	*phac, phak*
less	*mi*
less	*min*
letter	*liter*

lid	*opercul*
to lie (down)	*cumb, cub*
to lie	*pseud*
to lie open	*pat, pass*
life	*anima*
life	*bio*
life	*lif*
life	*spir*
life	*vita*
life	*-zoic*
to lift	*aort*
to lift	*hev*
ligament	*des, dem*
light (in weight)	*elaphr*
light (in weight)	*lev*
light	*liht*
light	*luc*
light	*lumin*
light	*phot, phos*
lightning	*ceraun, keraun*
like	*-al*
like	*-an*
like	*-ane*
like	*-ar*
like	*-ary*
like	*-cund, -und*
like	*-ent*
like	*-eous*
like	*-ese*
like	*-ic*
like	*-ical*

like	*-id*
like	*-ile*
like	*-ine*
like	*-ish*
like	*lik*
like	*-ory*
like	*simil*
lily	*crin*
limb	*mel*
limb	*membr*
lime	*calc*
limit	*fin*
line	*line*
line	*stich*
linen	*byss*
lion	*leon*
lip	*cheil, chil*
lip	*labi, labr*
liquid	*hum*
(watery) liquid	*ser*
little	*-cle, -cule*
little	*-ek, -ik*
little	*-el*
little	*-ette, -et*
little	*-kin*
little	*lept*
little	*-let*
little	*-ling*
little	*micro-*
little	*min*
little	*-ock*

little	*parv*
little	*paul*
little	*petit*
little	*-ule, -ula*
little	*-y, -ie*
to live	*bio*
to live	*lif*
to live	*viv*
lively	*vig*
liver	*hepat*
lizard	*saur*
to load	*charg*
loaf (bread)	*laf*
lobe	*lob*
loin	*lumb*
long	*dolicho-*
long	*long*
to look	*blep*
to look	*spec, spic*
to look	*scop*
to look at	*-orama*
to look at	*show*
to look at	*skep*
to look at	*the*
to look at	*tu*
loose	*lack*
loose	*lax*
loose	*leas, laiss*
to loose	*lys, lyt*
to loose	*solv, solu*
to lose	*los*

loss	*damn*
lot	*cler*
lot	*sort*
louse	*pedicul*
love	*agap*
to love	*am*
to love	*ero*
to love	*fre*
to love	*phil*
low	*bass*
low	*chamae*
lump	*chalaz*
lung	*pneumon, pneum, pne*
lung	*pulm, pulmon*
lust	*-lagnia*

M

machine	*mechan*
Magnesia (in Thessaly)	*magnes, magnet*
maiden	*nymph*
to make	*-ate*
to make	*be-*
to make	*creat*
to make	*-en*
to make	*fac, fic, fect, -fy*
to make	*-ize, -ise*
to make	*mak*
to make	*poie, poe*
to make certain	*cern, cert*

man	*andr*
man	*anthrop*
man	*carl*
man	*homo*
man	*man*
man	*mascul*
man	*vir*
manly	*arsen*
manner	*mod*
in the manner of	*-atim*
in the manner of	*-esque*
in the manner of	*-ly*
in the manner of	*-wise*
mantle	*palli*
mantle	*tunic*
many	*multi-*
many	*myria-*
many	*poly-*
how many	*quot*
mark	*macul*
mark	*stib*
to mark	*stig, sting, stinct*
marketplace	*agor*
marriage	*gam*
marrow	*medull*
marrow	*myel*
to marry	*junct, jug, join*
to marry	*nub, nupt*
Mars (Ares)	*areo*
Mars	*mar*
mask	*larv*

Mass (ceremony)	*-mas*
mass	*onc*
master	*domin*
mating	*gam*
mating	*junct, jug, join*
matter	*hyl, yl*
mature	*fledge*
mature	*pub*
maze	*labyrinth*
meadow	*-ley*
meaning	*sem*
to measure	*mens*
to measure	*met*
measure	*meter, metr*
measure	*mod*
measured flow	*rhythm*
meat	*carn*
meat	*creat, cre-, kre-*
meat	*met*
meat	*sarc*
to meet	*met*
member	*membr*
fetal membrane	*chori*
membrane	*hymen*
membrane	*mening*
membrane	*myring*
Mercury	*mercur*
merry	*hilar*
message	*angel*
messenger	*angel*
metal plate	*elasm*

middle	*med*
middle	*meso-*
middle	*mezz-*
Milan (Italy)	*milan*
mild	*leni*
mildew	*mucedin*
milk	*galact*
milk	*lac*
million	*mega-, megal-, meg-*
mind	*ment*
mind	*psych*
miracle	*thaum*
mite	*acar*
to mix	*misc*
to mix	*mix*
to mix	*mong*
mixing	*cras*
proper mixture	*temper*
mob	*demo-*
mob	*ochlo-*
mob	*pleb*
mob	*vulg*
model	*typ*
to be modest	*pud*
mold	*eurot*
moldy	*muc*
money	*ſe*
money	*lucr*
money	*pecu*
monster	*terat*
month	*men*

month	*mens*
month	*-mester*
moon	*lun*
moon	*men*
moon	*mens*
moon	*mon*
moon	*selen*
more	*-er*
more	*ple, plei*
more	*plus, plur*
moss	*bry*
most	*-est*
mother	*mater*
mother	*metr*
mountain	*-berg*
mountain	*mount, mont*
mouse	*mus*
mouse	*my*
mouth	*bucc*
mouth (of river)	*-mouth*
mouth	*or, os*
mouth	*stom*
to move	*kine-, cinema-*
to move	*mov, mot, mob*
how much	*quant*
mucus	*blenn*
mucus	*muc*
mucus	*myx*
muscle	*mus*
muscle	*my*
Muse	*mus*

mussel	*mytil*
to mutilate	*maym*
mutually	*allel*
my	*mon-, ma-*
mystery	*myst*

N

nail	*clav*
(finger-)nail	*onych*
naked	*gym*
naked	*nud*
name	*nam*
name	*nomin, nom*
name	*onym, onoma*
narrow	*angust*
narrow	*sten*
nation	*ethn*
nation	*gen*
natural	*physi*
nature	*physi*
navel	*omphal*
navel	*umbilic*
near	*engy-*
near	*neigh*
near	*prox*
neck	*cervic*
neck	*coll*
neck	*trachel*
need	*ned*
to need	*-penia*
negative	*a-, an-*

negative	*de-*
negative	*dis-, di-, dif-*
negative	*in-, il-, im-, ir-*
negative	*n-*
negative	*ne-*
negative	*non-*
negative	*un-*
neighbor	*vicin*
neither	*neutr*
nephew	*nepot*
Neptune	*neptun*
nerve	*nerv*
nerve	*neur*
nest	*nid*
net	*dicty, dikty*
net	*ret*
nettle	*cnid*
new	*cen, caen, -cene*
new	*neo-*
new	*nov*
next to	*juxta-*
nickel	*nickel*
night	*niht*
night	*noc, nox*
night	*nyct*
nine	*ennea-*
nine	*novem, non*
nipple	*papill*
nipple	*thel*
niter	*nitr*
nitrogen	*nitr*

(dull) noise	*bomb*
noon	*meridi*
no-place	*utop*
north	*arct*
north	*boreal*
north	*hyperbor*
north	*nor-*
north	*septentrion*
nose	*nas, nar*
nose	*nos*
nose	*rhin*
not	*a-, an-*
not	*de-*
not	*dis-, di-, dif-*
not	*in-, il-, im-, ir-*
not	*n-*
not	*ne-*
not	*non-*
not	*un-*
notch	*scor*
nothing	*nul, nihil*
to nourish	*al*
to nourish	*nutri*
to nourish	*troph*
nucleus	*kary, cary*
numb	*torp*
number	*arithm*
number	*numer*
numbness	*narc*
nut	*kary, cary*
nut	*nucle*

O

oak	*rob*
oar	*rem*
oblique	*lox*
oblique	*obliqu*
oblique	*plagi*
petty obstacle	*tric*
to obstruct	*cumber*
obstruction	*barr*
offspring	*prol*
oil	*ole, -ol*
to oil	*unct, oint*
old	*ger*
old	*presby*
old	*sen*
old	*vet*
(Mt.) Olympus	*olymp*
on	*a-*
on	*epi-, ep-*
one	*hen*
one	*mono-*
one	*uni-*
one-and-one-half	*sesqui-*
one who	*-aire, -air*
one who	*-an, -ian*
one who	*-ant*
one who	*-ar*
one who	*-ard, -art*
one who	*-ary*
one who	*-ast*

one who	*-ate*
one who (passive)	*-ee*
one who	*-eer*
one who	*-ent*
one who	*-er, -yer*
one who	*-ero*
one who	*-eur*
one who	*-ier*
one who	*-ist*
one who	*-ite*
one who	*-ive*
one who	*-nik*
one who	*-or*
one who	*-ster*
to open	*apert*
opening	*chasm*
opening	*for*
opening	*foramin*
opening	*lumin*
opening	*osti*
opening	*por*
opening	*stom*
opening	*trema*
opinion	*dog, dox*
opium	*opi*
opposite	*anti-, ant-*
opposite	*contra-, counter-*
orange	*fulv*
orange	*rutil*
order	*nom*
order	*ordin*

other	*all*
other	*alter, al*
other	*hetero-*
out	*ab-*
out	*apo-, ap-*
out	*cata-, cath-, cat-*
out	*de-*
out	*dis-, di-, dif-*
out	*e-, ex-*
out	*ec-*
out	*out-*
out	*ut*
outdoors	*for*
outer	*ecto-*
outside	*ecto-*
outside	*epi-, ep-*
outside	*exo-*
outside	*exter-*
outside	*extra-*
outward	*extra-*
over	*hyper-*
over	*super-, supra-, sur-*
to owe	*deb*
one's own	*idio-*
one's own	*propr*
ox	*bou, bov*

P

| pain | *alg* |
| pain | *odyn* |

painful	*sor*
to paint	*pict*
paired	*zyg, zeug*
pale	*blanc*
pale	*bleach*
pale	*ochr*
pale	*pal*
Pallas	*pallad*
pan	*patell*
paper	*cart*
paralysis	*pleg*
part	*deal*
part	*mer*
part	*part*
passage	*por*
to pat	*palp*
path	*path*
pause	*paul*
pause	*paus*
to pay	*pend, pens*
peace	*pac*
pear	*pyr*
pearl	*margarit*
peasant	*bor*
pebble	*calcul*
pen	*styl*
penis	*balan*
penis	*pen*
penis	*phall*
people	*demo*
people	*folk*

people	*la*
people	*ochlo-*
people	*pleb*
people	*popul*
people	*vulg*
to perceive	*cern, cert*
perforated	*ethm*
perforation	*cente*
to perform	*funct*
permissible	*lic*
Persian	*persic*
personal	*idio-*
personal	*propr*
to persuade	*suad, suas*
phlegm	*pituit*
phylum	*phyl*
to pierce	*broc*
to pierce	*stik*
to pierce	*thrill*
pigeon	*columb*
pillar	*cion*
pin	*fibul*
pinecone	*pin*
pinecone	*strobil*
pipe	*aul*
pipe	*solen*
pipe	*syring*
pipe	*tub*
pit	*alveol*
place	*loc*
to place	*pon, pos*

place	*stall*
place	*stead*
to place	*thes, thet*
place	*top*
place where	*-ary, -arium*
place where	*-ery*
place where	*-ory, -orium*
plague	*pest*
plank	*tabl*
plant	*phyt*
thin plate	*petal*
platinum	*platin*
to play	*lud, lus*
to please	*plac*
pleased	*grat*
pleasure	*hedon*
to pledge	*spond, spons*
plowshare	*vomer*
to pluck	*tes*
plumb-line	*plumb*
to plunge	*merg, mers*
Pluto	*plut*
point	*cuspid*
pointer	*indic*
poison	*tox*
poison	*venen*
poison	*vir*
to polish	*pol*
Polish	*pol*
pollution	*miasm*
pollution	*mys*

pool	*limn*
pool	*stagn*
poplar	*alam*
portion	*cler*
potash	*potass*
potassium	*potass*
to pound	*tus*
to pour	*chem*
to pour	*fus, fund, found*
power	*dyn, dynam*
power	*erg, urg*
having the power of	*-ive*
pox	*variol*
praise	*dog, dox*
to pray	*bid, bead*
to pray	*ora*
to pray	*prec*
precious	*dear*
to prepare	*par*
to press	*press, print*
to press together	*arct*
to press together	*stip*
pressure	*bar*
to prevent	*para*
price	*preci*
to prick	*pung, punct*
to prick	*stig, sting, stinct*
to proclaim	*ban*
to produce	*poie, poe*
profit	*lucr*
to project	*min*

projecting	*glochi*
Prometheus	*prometh*
proper	*dec*
property	*fe*
property	*pecu*
prostitute	*porn*
to protect	*alex*
to protect	*gar*
to protect	*ward*
to protect	*warn*
provident	*prometh*
prow	*rostr*
to prune	*put*
pubic	*pub*
pug-nosed	*sim*
to pull	*tract*
pulley	*troch*
pulse	*sphygm*
puncture	*cente*
puncture	*nyx*
puncture	*pung, punct*
to punish	*pun*
punishment	*pen*
pupil (eye)	*cor*
pure	*cast*
pure	*cath, kath*
purple	*purpur*
to pursue	*hunt*
pus	*py*
to push	*pel, puls*
to push	*shuf*

pushing	*osm*
to put	*pon, pos*
to put	*thes, thet*
putrid	*sapr*
putrid	*seps, sept*
puzzle	*enigm*

Q

having the quality of	*-aceous*
having the quality of	*-acious*
quality	*-acity*
quality	*-acy, -cy*
quality	*-age*
quality	*-ance*
quality	*-ancy*
quality	*-aneity, -eity*
having the quality of	*-aneous*
quality	*-asia, -asis*
quality	*-asm*
having the quality of	*-ate*
quality	*-dom*
having the quality of	*-en*
quality	*-ence*
quality	*-ency*
having the quality of	*-eous*
quality	*-ery, -ry*
quality	*-esis*
quality	*-ety*
having the quality of	*-ful*

quality	*-hood*
quality	*-ion, -tion*
quality	*-ism*
having the quality of	*-ite*
having the quality of	*-itious*
quality	*-ity*
having the quality of	*-ly*
quality	*-ment*
quality	*-mony*
quality	*-ness*
having the quality of	*-orious*
having the quality of	*-ory*
having the quality of	*-ose*
having the quality of	*-otic*
having the quality of	*-ous*
having the quality of	*-ow*
quality	*-ship*
quality	*-th*
quality	*-tude*
quality	*-ty*
having the quality of	*-ulent*
having the quality of	*-ulous*
having the quality of	*-uous*
quality	*-ure*
quality	*-y*
having the quality of	*-y*

R

rabies	*rab*
race	*ethn*

race	*gen*
race	*phyl*
rain	*hyet*
rain	*ombr*
rain	*pluvi*
rainbow	*irid*
to raise	*lev*
to raise	*tol*
a ram	*cri*
in ranks	*phalang*
raven	*corac*
ray	*actin*
ray	*rad*
to read	*leg, lig, lect*
to read	*-lexia*
to reason	*rat*
recent	*cen, caen, -cene*
to recite	*spell*
to reckon	*rat*
red	*erythr*
red	*phoenic*
red	*red*
red	*rhod*
red	*ros*
red	*rub*
red	*ruf*
red	*rutil*
reed	*calam*
reed	*can*
to relate	*tell, tal*
related to	*-ac, -iac*

related to	*-al*
related to	*-an*
related to	*-ane*
related to	*-ar*
related to	*-ary*
related to	*-cund, -und*
related to	*-ent*
related to	*-eous*
related to	*-ern*
related to	*-ese*
related to	*-ic*
related to	*-ical*
related to	*-id*
related to	*-ile*
related to	*-ine*
related to	*-ish*
related to	*-ite*
related to	*-otic*
relative	*sib*
to remember	*memor*
to remember	*mne*
to remind	*moni*
reproductive	*gono-*
resemblance	*eido-*
resembling	*-oid, -oda, -ode*
to rest	*quies, quiet*
result	*-em*
result	*-eme*
result	*-ma*
result	*-men*

result	-y
a revel	com
Rhine	rhen
rib	cost
rib	pleur
ribbon	taen
to ride	rid
right	orth-
right	rect
right	reg
right hand	dextr
rind	lemm
ring	an
ring	annel, annul
ring	cortic
ring	cric
ring	gyr
ring	sphincter
ripe	ripe
to rise	ori, ort
to rise	ris
rising	orient
river	guad
river	potam
road	od, hod
road	via
to rob	rob, rev
rock	lapid
rock	-lite
rock	lith
rock	petr

rock	*sax*
rock	*ston, stan*
rod	*can*
rod	*rhabd*
to roll	*roll, rol*
to roll	*volv, volu*
Roman	*roman*
roof	*steg*
room	*cell*
root	*radic*
root	*rhiz*
rope	*fun*
rose	*ros*
rotten	*putr*
rough	*asper*
rough	*trachy*
round	*circul*
royal	*basil*
royal	*reg*
to rub	*fric*
to rub	*trip, trib*
to rub	*trit*
to rule	*arch*
a rule	*can*
to rule	*-crat, crac*
a rule	*norm*
to rule	*rect*
to rule	*reg*
rump	*glute*
rump	*pyg*
to run	*cur, course*

to run	*drom*
to run	*leap*
to run	*run*
runner	*trochanter*
Russia	*russ*
Russia	*ruthen*

S

S	*sigm*
sack	*burs*
sack	*pock*
sacred	*hier*
sacred	*sacr*
safe	*salv*
safety	*soter*
to sail	*naut*
to sail	*nav*
saint	*san, sant*
saliva	*ptyal*
saliva	*sial*
a salt	*hal*
salt	*sal*
salvation	*soter*
same	*homo-*
same	*ident*
same	*tauto-*
sand	*aren*
Sardinia	*sardin*
Saturn	*saturn*
sausage	*botul*

a saw	*serrat, serr*
(made by Adolphe) Sax	*sax*
Saxons	*-sex*
to say	*dict*
to say	*phe, phas*
scale	*lep, lepid*
scale	*squam*
Scandinavia	*scand*
scar	*ul*
science	*-ics*
to scrape	*ras, rad*
to scrape	*scrap*
to scream	*gal*
sea	*mar*
sea	*pelag*
sea	*thalass, thalatt*
seal	*bull*
seal (animal)	*phoc*
seashore	*littor*
seat	*hedr*
second	*deuter*
to see	*blep*
to see	*id, eid*
to see	*op*
to see	*-orama*
to see	*scop*
to see	*see*
to see	*spec, spic*
to see	*vid, vis*
seed	*semin*
seed	*sperm*

seed	*spor*
to seek	*petit*
to seek	*quest, quir, quis*
to seem	*think*
to seize	*cap, cip, cept, ceive*
to seize	*empt*
to seize	*grip*
to seize	*hunt*
to seize	*lab, lept*
to seize	*prehend, prehens, pris*
to seize	*sum, sumpt*
to seize	*rap*
seizure	*agra*
self	*auto-*
self	*ego*
self	*sui*
to sell	*poly*
to sell	*sell*
to sell	*vend*
to send	*mit, miss*
to send	*stol, stal, -stle*
to separate	*crin*
separate	*priv*
separated	*chorist*
series	*ser*
serious	*sever*
to serve	*minister*
to serve	*serv*
service	*mun*
(stage-) set	*scen*
to set	*sist*

to set	*sit, set*
to set	*sta, stit*
to set up	*stor*
seven	*hept-*
seven	*sept-*
to sew	*raph, raphid, -rrhaph*
sewer	*cloac*
sexual	*vener*
shade	*shad*
shade	*umbr*
shadow	*sci, ski*
shaggy	*rugh*
shaggy	*vill*
to shake	*seism*
to shake	*shake*
to shake	*trem, trom*
shank	*crur*
shape	*form*
shape	*morph*
to share	*trib*
sharp	*ac, acr*
sharp	*oxy*
to shear	*tons*
sheath	*cole*
sheath	*vagin*
sheet	*lamin, lamell*
small sheet	*nap*
shell	*cochl*
shell	*conch*
shell	*ostrac*
shelter	*burg*

shield	*aspid*
shield	*clype*
shield	*scut*
shield	*thyr*
shinbone	*cnem*
shinbone	*tibi*
to shine	*shin*
to shine	*splend*
ship	*nav*
shoe	*calce*
to shoot	*shot*
short	*brachy-*
short	*brev*
shoulder-blade	*scapul*
to shout	*clam, claim*
to show	*phan, phen*
to show	*tech*
sickle	*falc*
side	*cost*
side	*hedr*
side	*later*
side	*pleur*
side	*side*
sieve	*ethm*
sight	*op*
sigma-shaped (S)	*sigm*
sign	*beck*
sign	*mark*
sign	*sem*
sign	*sign*
silent	*tac, tic*

silicon	*silic*
silk	*seric*
silver	*argent*
silver	*argyr*
silver	*platin*
similar	*lik*
to sing	*gal*
to sing	*sing*
single	*haplo-*
single	*mono-*
single	*priv*
single	*uni-*
sinus	*antr*
sinus	*sinus, sinu*
sister	*soror*
to sit	*sed, sid, sess*
to sit	*sit, set*
six	*hexa-*
six	*sex-*
skill	*art*
skill	*techn*
skin	*chori*
skin	*cut*
skin	*derm*
skin	*lemm*
skin	*pel*
skull	*crani*
sky	*cel*
sky	*uran*
slave	*thrall*
Slavic	*slav*

to slay	*sla*
to sleep	*com*
to sleep	*dorm*
sleep	*hypn*
sleep	*somn*
to slide	*slid*
to slip	*lapse*
slippery	*lubr*
slope	*clin, climat*
slow	*brady-*
slow	*lent*
slow	*slow*
slow	*tard*
small	*-cle, -cule*
small	*-ek, -ik*
small	*-el*
small	*-ette, -et*
small	*-kin*
small	*lept*
small	*-let*
small	*-ling*
small	*micro-*
small	*min*
small	*-ock*
small	*parv*
small	*paul*
small	*petit*
small	*-ule, -ula*
small	*-y, -ie*
smallest	*minim*
smell	*od*

smell	*osm*
smell	*osphr*
smelling	*olfact*
smoke	*capn*
smoke	*fum*
smooth	*leio-, lio*
smooth	*lev*
snake	*angui*
snake	*colubr*
snake	*herpet*
snake	*ophi, ophidi*
to snare	*lic*
to snatch	*rap*
snout	*rhynch*
snow	*chion, chio*
snow	*niv*
snub-nosed	*sim*
soap	*sap*
soda	*sod*
sodium	*sod*
soft	*leni*
soft	*malac*
soft	*moll*
soft (sound)	*plan*
sole (of foot)	*plant*
solid	*solid*
solid	*stereo-, ster*
son	*fil*
son of	*bar-*
son of	*ben-*
son of	*-ez*

son of	*fitz-*
son of	*mac-, mc-*
son of	*-poulos*
son of	*-s*
son of	*-son, -sen*
son of	*-vich*
song	*cant*
song	*mel*
song	*od*
sooner	*ere*
soothsayer	*augur*
soul	*anima*
soul	*psych*
sound	*ech*
sound	*phon*
sound	*phthong*
sound	*son*
sour	*acid*
sour	*sour*
south	*austral*
south	*meridi*
south	*noto-*
south	*su-*
to sow	*spor*
space	*are*
space	*lacun*
Spanish	*hispan, span*
spark	*scintill*
spasm	*clon*
to speak	*dict*
to speak	*fa, fess*

to speak	*loqu, loc*
to speak	*ora*
to speak	*phe, phas*
to speak	*spek*
spear	*ger*
speech	*lex*
speech	*parl*
speech	*phras*
sphere	*glob*
spider	*arachn*
to spin	*rhomb*
to spin	*spin*
to spin	*turbin*
spine	*acanth*
spine	*rach, rrhach*
spine	*spin*
spiny	*echin*
spiral	*helic*
spirit	*anima*
spirit	*spir*
spirit	*thym*
spittle	*ptyal*
spleen	*lien*
spleen	*splen*
to split	*cleav*
to split	*fiss, -fid*
to split	*schiz, schis*
sponge	*spong*
spoon	*cochl*
spot	*macul*
spread	*patul*

to spread	*strat*
spring	*-burn, -brunn*
to sprout	*blast*
sprout	*clad*
small staff	*bacill*
small staff	*bacter*
stain	*macul*
stalk	*caul*
to stand	*sist*
to stand	*sta, stit*
standing	*stasis, stat*
star	*aster, astr*
star	*sider*
star	*stell*
starch	*amyl*
state	*-acy, -cy*
state	*-age*
state	*-ance*
state	*-ancy*
state	*-asia, -asis*
state	*-asm*
state	*-dom*
state	*-ence*
state	*-ency*
state	*-ery, -ry*
state	*-esis*
state	*-ety*
state	*-hood*
state	*-ion, -tion*
state	*-ism*
state	*-ity*

state	*-ment*
state	*-mony*
state	*-ness*
state (polity)	*poli, polit*
state	*-ship*
state	*-th*
state	*-tude*
state	*-ty*
state	*-ure*
state	*-y*
to stay	*bide*
to stay	*man*
to steal	*klept*
steam	*vap*
to steer	*ster*
stem	*stip*
stem	*stirp*
stench	*brom*
to step	*grad, gress*
to stick	*clam*
to stick	*cleav*
to stick	*her, hes*
sticky	*muc*
sticky	*visc*
stiff	*star*
to stink	*fet*
stirrup-bone	*staped*
to stitch	*broc*
stock	*stirp*
stomach	*gastr*
stomach	*ventr*

stone	*lapid*
stone	*-lite*
stone	*lith*
stone	*petr*
stone	*sax*
stone	*-stein*
stone	*ston, stan*
straight	*euthy-*
straight	*orth-*
straight	*rect*
straight	*reg*
strange	*xen*
stranger	*barbar*
stranger	*wal*
straw	*carph*
to stretch	*rec*
to stretch	*strec*
to stretch	*tend, tens, tent*
stretched tight	*ten, tenon*
stretching	*ton, ta, tetan*
to strew	*spers*
to strike	*bat*
to strike	*coup*
to strike	*cuss*
to strike	*fend*
to strike	*flict*
to strike	*plaud*
to strike	*plex, pless*
to strike	*sla*
string	*chord*
stroke	*pleg*

strong	*firm*
strong	*fort*
strong	*rob*
strong	*sthen*
to be strong	*val*
Strontian (in Scotland)	*stront*
strontium	*stront*
struggle	*agon*
to struggle	*luct*
study of	*-logy, -ology*
to stuff	*farc*
stumbling-block	*scandal*
stupid	*mor*
stupid	*stult*
stupor	*carotid*
stupor	*narc*
stupor	*stup*
stupor	*torp*
stupor	*typh*
substance	*hyl, yl*
substitute	*vic*
to suffer	*pat, pass*
suffering	*path*
sugar	*sacchar*
sulfur	*sulf, sulph*
sulfur	*thi*
sum	*summ*
to summon	*cit*
sun	*heli*
sun	*sol*
superior	*magister*

to supply	*gar*
to support	*tol*
suture	*raph, raphid, -rrhaph*
to swear	*jur*
to swear	*swer*
sweat	*hidr*
sweat	*sud*
sweet	*dulc*
sweet	*glyc, gluc*
sweet	*suav*
sweet	*swet*
to swell	*bel*
to swell	*blaw*
to swell	*bry*
to swell	*edema*
to swell	*tum*
swelling	*tuber*
to swim	*nect*
to swing	*oscill*
sword	*ens*
sword	*gladi*
sword	*xiph*
system	*-ics*

T

table	*mens*
tail	*caud*
tail	*cerc*
tail	*pen*
tail	*ur*

to take	*cap, cip, cept, ceive*
to take	*empt*
to take	*grip*
to take	*hunt*
to take	*lab, lep*
to take	*prehend, prehens, pris*
to take	*rap*
to take	*sum, sumpt*
tale	*ep*
to talk	*lal*
tanbark	*tann*
Tantalus	*tantal*
to tap (keg)	*broc*
tapeworm	*taen*
taste	*gust*
taste	*sap*
tawny	*fusc*
to teach	*doc*
to teach	*lern*
tear(-drop)	*dacry*
tear(-drop)	*lacrim, lachrym*
tellurium	*tellur*
ten	*dec, deka*
ten	*ten*
ten and	*-teen*
times ten	*-ty*
tender	*pi*
tending toward	*-bund, -bond*
ten thousand	*myria-*
terrible	*din, dein*
to terrify	*gast*

to test	*prob*
testicle	*orchid*
testicle	*test*
thallium	*thall*
thankful	*grat*
thanks	*charis*
that which	*-acle*
that which	*-aire, -air*
that which	*-ant*
that which	*-ate*
that which	*-ent*
that which	*-er*
that which	*-ero*
that which	*-ive*
that which	*-ment*
that which	*-mony*
that which	*-or*
that which	*-th*
that which	*-ty*
that which	*-ure*
the	*al-*
there	*ibi*
thick	*pachy-*
thick	*pycn*
thigh	*femor*
thigh	*mer*
thin	*lept*
thin	*mac*
thin	*tenu*
thing	*re*
thirst	*dips*

thirst	*thirst*
on this side	*cis-, citra-*
Thor	*thor*
thorn	*acanth*
thorn	*spin*
thoroughly	*be-*
thoroughly	*cata-, cath-, cat-*
thoroughly	*com-, co-, col-, con-, cor-*
thoroughly	*en-, em-*
thoroughly	*per-, pel-*
thousand	*kilo-, chilio-*
thousand	*milli-*
thread	*fil*
thread	*mit*
thread	*nemat*
three	*ter*
three	*tri-*
three-dimensional	*stereo-, ster*
threshold	*limin*
throat	*gorg*
throat	*guttur*
throat	*pharyng*
through	*dia-, di-*
through	*per-, pel-*
to throw	*bol, ball*
to throw	*ject, jac*
to throw	*lanc*
to throw	*shot*
to thrust	*trud, trus*
thunder	*bront*
thymus gland	*thym*

thyroid	*thyr*
tibia	*cnem*
to tie	*string, strict*
to till	*col, cult*
time	*chron*
time	*ev*
time	*tempor*
time of	*-ice*
times	*-fold*
times	*-ple*
tin	*stann*
tissue	*hist*
titan	*titan*
to	*ad-*
to	*ob-, oc-, of-, op-*
to be done	*-end, -and*
toe	*digit*
together	*com-, co-, col, con-, cor-*
together	*syn-, syl-, sym-, sys-, sy-*
tomb	*taph*
tone	*ton, ta, tetan*
tongue	*gloss, glot*
tongue	*lingu*
tonsil	*amygdal*
too much	*over-*
tooth	*dent*
tooth	*odont*
top	*apic*
torch	*blaz*
to touch	*hapt, haph, aph, apse*
to touch	*tang, tact*

to touch	*thigma*
toward	*ad-*
toward	*ob-, oc-, of-, op-*
toward	*-ward*
tower	*turr*
town	*-abad*
town	*burg*
town	*-burg, -burgh*
town	*-bury, -borough*
town	*-by*
town	*-dorf, -thorpe*
town	*ham, -heim, home*
town	*-ton*
town	*-ville*
town	*-wich, -wick*
to trade	*merc*
to transport	*perei*
treatment	*therapy*
tree	*dendr*
tribe	*phyl*
trillion	*treg*
trough	*pyel*
true	*etym*
true	*soth*
true	*ver*
trumpet	*salping*
to try	*tempt*
to try out	*per*
tube	*can*
tube	*salping*
tube	*siphon*

tube	*solen*
tube	*syring*
tube	*tub*
to tug	*vuls*
tumor	*-cele*
tumor	*-oma*
tumor	*onc*
Turkey	*turk*
to turn	*rot*
to turn	*stroph, streph, strept*
to turn	*trop*
to turn	*vert, vers*
to turn	*warf*
in turns	*vic*
twelve	*dodeca-*
twelve	*duodec-, duoden-*
twig	*thall*
twin	*didym*
twin	*gemin*
to twist	*tor*
to twist	*wring*
to twist	*writh*
twisted	*plect*
twisted	*strobil*
two	*bi-*
two	*di-*
two	*dicho-*
two	*du-*
two	*dy-*
two	*twi-*
tyrant	*tyrann*

U

uncovered	*gym*
uncovered	*nud*
under	*hypo-, hyp-*
under	*neth*
under	*sub-, suc-, suf-, sug-, sup-, sur-*
under	*under-*
universe	*cosm*
up	*ana-*
upper air	*ether*
upsilon-shaped (U)	*hyo-*
urine	*ur, uret*
urine	*urin*
use	*chres*
to use	*us, ut*
uterus	*hyster*
uterus	*metr*
uterus	*uter*
uvula	*cion*

V

vagina	*colp*
vagina	*vagin*
valley	*dal, tal*
valley	*val*
value	*worth*
Vanadis (goddess)	*vanad*

variation	*para-, par-*
vehicle	*car*
veil	*vel*
vein	*phleb*
(dilated) vein	*varic*
vein	*ven*
velvet	*vill*
vertebra	*spondyl*
vertebra	*vertebr*
vessel	*angi*
vessel	*vas*
view	*-orama*
vinegar	*acet*
violet	*iod, ion*
violet	*porphyr*
violet	*violac*
virgin	*parthen*
virus	*vir*
viscera	*splanchn*
visible	*phaner*
voice	*phthong*
voice	*voc, voke*
to vomit	*emet*
to vow	*vot*
Vulcan	*vulcan*

W

to walk	*ambul*
wall	*mur*

wall	*pariet*
wall	*sept*
to wander	*err*
to wander	*migra*
to wander	*plan*
to wander	*vag*
to want	*desider*
war	*bell*
war	*guerr*
to warn	*moni*
wart	*verruc*
to wash	*lav, lu*
to waste away	*phthis*
wasteland	*heath*
wasting	*tab*
watchman	*gregor*
water	*aqua*
water	*hydat*
water	*hydr*
clear water	*lymph*
wave	*kym, cym*
wave	*und*
wax	*cer*
way	*via*
wealth	*plut*
weapon	*arm*
weapon	*opl*
to wear	*wer*
to weave	*text*
wedge	*cune*

wedge	*sphen*
week	*hebdomad*
to weigh	*grav*
to weigh	*pend, pens*
weight	*bar*
weight	*liber, libr*
weight	*ponder*
well	*bene-*
well	*eu-*
well-born	*gen*
west	*hesper*
west	*occident*
westwind	*zephyr*
wet	*hygr*
whale	*balaen*
whale	*cet*
wheel	*rot*
wheel	*troch*
whip	*flagell*
whirling	*din*
white	*alb*
white	*blanc*
white	*bleach*
white	*cand*
white	*leuc, leuk*
white	*weiss*
whole	*hal*
whole	*hol*
whole	*integr*
wide	*brad*

wide	*eury-*
wide	*lat*
wife	*uxor*
to will	*bul*
to will	*vol*
willow	*salic*
wind	*anem*
wind	*vent*
windbag	*foll*
window	*fenestra*
windpipe	*bronch*
windpipe	*laryng*
windpipe	*trache*
wine	*methy*
wine	*oen, en*
wine	*vin*
wing	*ala*
wing	*pter*
winking	*nictitat*
winter	*hibern*
wisdom	*sap*
wise	*soph*
with	*com-, co-, col-, con-, cor-*
with	*syn-, syl-, sym-, sys-, sy-*
within	*ento-*
within	*eso-*
within	*indi-*
within	*int-*
within	*intro-, intra-*
without	*a-, an-*

without	*-less*
without	*sine*
witness	*martyr*
witness	*test*
wolf	*lup*
wolf	*lyc*
woman	*dam*
woman	*femin*
woman	*gyn*
woman who	*-ster*
womb	*hyster*
womb	*metr*
womb	*uter*
to wonder	*mir*
wonder	*thaum*
wood	*hyl, yl*
wood	*lign*
wood	*xyl*
wool	*lan*
word	*ep*
word	*lex*
word	*log*
word	*parl*
word	*verb*
work	*erg, urg*
to work	*labor*
work	*oper*
to work	*wroht*
worker	*smith*
world	*mund*

worm	*helminth*
worm	*scolec*
worm	*verm*
worship	*-latry*
worthy	*dign*
wound	*traumat*
wound	*vuln*
wreath	*coron*
wretched	*miser*
wrinkle	*rhyt, rut*
wrinkle	*rug*
wrist	*carp*
to write	*graph, gram*
to write	*scrib, script*

Y

year	*ann, enn*
yellow	*flav*
yellow	*chrys*
yellow	*cirr, cirrh*
yellow	*lute*
yellow	*ochr*
yellow	*xanth*
to yield	*cede, ceed, cess*
yoke	*zyg, zeug*
yolk	*lecith*
yolk	*vitell*
young	*hebe*

young	*juven, jun*
Ytterby (in Sweden)	*ytterb*

Z

zinc	*zinc*
zircon	*zircon*

PART TWO

EXERCISES

THE SOURCES OF ENGLISH

English belongs to a very large group of languages which is usually called the Indo-European family, taking its name from that of the earliest known member. Little is known about the Indo-European language or the people who spoke it except that it flourished about 2500 years before Christ and served as the source of most of the western languages in use today and many of the eastern as well.

English belongs to the Germanic branch of the Indo-European family, and specifically to the West Germanic branch from which modern German and Dutch are also descended. Thus a direct line can be traced from the language used by the early Germanic tribes of western Europe to the English language of today. In fact, it is only the words carried by the (Germanic) Anglo-Saxon invaders into Britain that can truly be called native English.

However, borrowing has played fully as large a part as direct inheritance in the shaping of English. The most important sources of borrowed words have been near relatives of the native tongue, other members of the same Indo-European family, notably Old Norse, Latin, French and Greek.

On the next few pages you will see in outline how English, through direct descent and copious borrowing, came to be the language we know today. On the first outline each of the major historical influences is shown, dated approximately, and numbered. The numbers on the outline above are repeated on the chart below where you will find a sample of the part of the English vocabulary affected by each event. The sources shown here have given us very nearly 100% of our language.

A second outline focuses on English alone and gives in greater detail the dates and events which have been important in the history of the language. Again, many of the dates are of necessity only approximate.

Together, these outlines help to explain the very diverse origins of the thousands of English word-roots listed in the dictionary above and presented again in a variety of ways for you to work with in the exercises which follow.

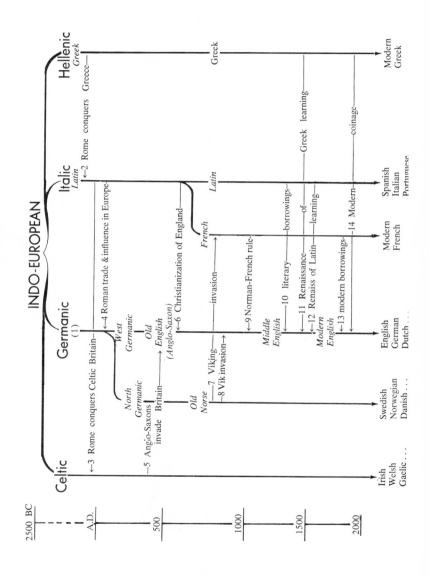

History	Line of Influence	Typical Words Involved
1. Direct descent	Germanic to Modern English	father, wife, child, house, eye, foot, eat, drink, stone, cow, road, lady, girdle
2. Roman conquest of Greece in 2nd C., B.C.	Greek to Latin	philosophy, history, geometry, school, crisis, atomic, meter, music, cynic, bishop, martyr
3. Roman occupation of Britain in 1st–5th C., A.D.	Latin to Celtic	port, (Man-, Win-, Dor-)chester, (War-)wick, (Nor-, Green-)wich
4. Roman military and commercial domination of Europe	Latin to Germanic	kitchen, cup, dish, butter, wine, cheese, pepper, street, mile, inch, Saturday, church
5. Germanic conquest of Celtic Britain after 449	Celtic to Old English (Anglo-Saxon)	York, Thames, London, Avon, Win(-chester), Wor(-cester), Salis(-bury), Cumberland
6. Systematic Christianization of England after 596	Latin to Old English (Anglo-Saxon)	altar, school, box, candle, noon, rule, meter, martyr, verse, priest, beet, radish, pear
7. Norse (Viking) invasion of France coast in 8–9th C.	Old Norse to French	see 8
8. Norse invasion of England in 8–9th C.	Old Norse to Old English	take, get, husband, sister, fellow, happy, law, leg, they, egg, steak, knife, window
9. Norman-French conquest of England in 1066	(Latin to) French to Middle English	nation, property, people, tax, money, city, army, very, nice, music, beef, soup, dinner
10. Direct literary borrowings in translations	Latin to Middle English	popular, quiet, history, nervous, polite, necessary, incredible, subdivide, ulcer
11. Direct, systematic borrowings during Renaissance	Greek to Early Modern English	poem, paragraph, scene, drama, theater, comedy, tragedy, anatomy, thermometer, climax, dialogue
12. Direct, systematic borrowings during Renaissance	Latin to Early Modern English	education, industry, position, item, exist, protest, solid, major, series, maturity
13. Modern borrowings	French to Modern English	machine, parade, garage, corsage, lingerie, divorcee, menu, omelet, casserole, grotesque
14. Modern coinage, largely in technical fields	Latin and Greek to Modern English	scientist, television, automobile, protein, radio, allergy, antibiotic, stereophonic

The Ages of English

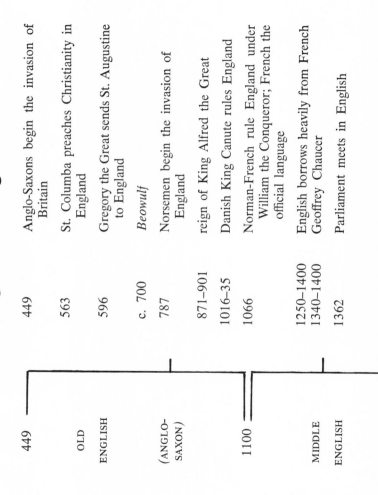

449	449	Anglo-Saxons begin the invasion of Britain
	563	St. Columba preaches Christianity in England
OLD ENGLISH	596	Gregory the Great sends St. Augustine to England
	c. 700	*Beowulf*
(ANGLO-SAXON)	787	Norsemen begin the invasion of England
	871–901	reign of King Alfred the Great
	1016–35	Danish King Canute rules England
1100	1066	Norman-French rule England under William the Conqueror; French the official language
MIDDLE ENGLISH	1250–1400 1340–1400	English borrows heavily from French Geoffrey Chaucer
	1362	Parliament meets in English

Date	Event	Period
1384	Wyclif's translation of the Bible	
1475	William Caxton introduces printing into England	
15th C.	East Midland (London) dialect becomes dominant	**1500**
16th C.	peak of the English Renaissance	EARLY MODERN ENGLISH
1564–1616	William Shakespeare	
1611	King James Version of the Bible	
17th C.	spread of the English language	**1700**
1755	Samuel Johnson's *Dictionary*	
18th C.	growth of American English	
1828	Noah Webster's *Dictionary* in America	
1928	completion of the *Oxford English Dictionary*	MODERN ENGLISH
20th C.	vast improvements in transportation, communication and technology; widespread borrowing and coinage of new words	

Latin Roots

Root	Meaning
1. **anima**	*spirit*
2. **ann, enn**	
3. **aqua**	
4. **audi**	
5. **cad, cid, cas**	
6. **cap, cip, cept, ceive**	
7. **capit**	
8. **-cide, cis**	
9. **clud, clus, claus, close**	
10. **cord**	
11. **corp**	
12. **cred**	
13. **dent**	
14. **dict**	
15. **duc**	
16. **fac, fic, fect, -fy**	
17. **fer**	
18. **frag, fract**	
19. **fug**	
20. **grad, gress**	
21. **ject, jac**	
22. **loqu, loc**	
23. **manu**	
24. **mater**	
25. **mit, miss**	

EXAMPLES

animal   animated   inanimate   unanimous

	Root	Meaning
26.	mort	
27.	mov, mot, mob	
28.	nat, nasc	
29.	nomin, nom	
30.	pater	
31.	pel, puls	
32.	pend, pens	
33.	plex, plic, ply	
34.	pon, pos	
35.	reg	
36.	scrib, script	
37.	sect, sec	
38.	sed, sid, sess	
39.	sequ, sec	
40.	sist	
41.	spec, spic	
42.	sta, stit	
43.	tor	
44.	tract	
45.	verb	
46.	vert, vers	
47.	vid, vis	
48.	viv	
49.	voc, voke	
50.	volv, volu	

EXAMPLES

Greek Roots

	Root	Meaning
1.	**anthrop**	*man, human being*
2.	**aster, astr**	
3.	**bibli**	
4.	**centr**	
5.	**chrom, chro**	
6.	**chron**	
7.	**cosm**	
8.	**-crat, crac**	
9.	**cycl**	
10.	**demo**	
11.	**dyn, dynam**	
12.	**erg, urg**	
13.	**esthet, esthes**	
14.	**gam**	
15.	**ge**	
16.	**gnos, gnom**	
17.	**gon**	
18.	**graph, gram**	
19.	**gyn**	
20.	**heli**	
21.	**hydr**	
22.	**iatr**	
23.	**kine-, cinema-**	
24.	**lith**	
25.	**log**	

EXAMPLES

anthropology   anthropoid   misanthrope

	ROOT	MEANING
26.	**-logy**	
27.	**mania**	
28.	**meter, metr**	
29.	**morph**	
30.	**nom**	
31.	**odont**	
32.	**onym, onoma**	
33.	**op**	
34.	**phan, phen**	
35.	**phil**	
36.	**phob**	
37.	**phon**	
38.	**phot, phos**	
39.	**pod, pus**	
40.	**poli, polit**	
41.	**scop**	
42.	**som, somat**	
43.	**soph**	
44.	**tax, tact**	
45.	**techn**	
46.	**the, theo**	
47.	**therm**	
48.	**thes, thet**	
49.	**top**	
50.	**trop**	

EXAMPLES

Anglo-Saxon (Old English) Roots

	Root	Meaning
1.	**ber**	*to carry, to bear*
2.	**bid, bead**	
3.	**bind**	
4.	**blaw**	
5.	**bleach**	
6.	**brek**	
7.	**brew**	
8.	**burn, bran**	
9.	**dear**	
10.	**drag**	
11.	**drif**	
12.	**drink**	
13.	**dryg**	
14.	**fare**	
15.	**fed**	
16.	**flot**	
17.	**fot, fet**	
18.	**hard, -ard**	
19.	**hel**	
20.	**hev**	
21.	**lack**	
22.	**laf**	
23.	**leap**	
24.	**led**	
25.	**lern**	

EXAMPLES

bear   berth   born   borne   burden   bore

	ROOT	MEANING
26.	**lik**	
27.	**los**	
28.	**mark**	
29.	**reck**	
30.	**rob, rev**	
31.	**say**	
32.	**shuf**	
33.	**side**	
34.	**sit, set**	
35.	**sla**	
36.	**spell**	
37.	**spin**	
38.	**stall**	
39.	**star**	
40.	**ster**	
41.	**swer**	
42.	**tell, tal**	
43.	**tes**	
44.	**tru**	
45.	**wak**	
46.	**ward**	
47.	**wit, wis**	
48.	**wring**	
49.	**writh**	
50.	**wroht**	

EXAMPLES

Prefixes

LATIN:

	PREFIX	MEANING
1.	**ab-**	*away, from*
2.	**ad-**	
3.	**ante-**	
4.	**circum-**	
5.	**com-**	
6.	**contra-, counter-**	
7.	**de-**	
8.	**dis-**	
9.	**e-, ex-**	
10.	**inter-**	
11.	**intro-, intra-**	
12.	**ob-**	
13.	**per-, pel-**	
14.	**post-**	
15.	**pre-, prae-**	
16.	**pro-**	
17.	**re-**	
18.	**se-**	
19.	**sub-**	
20.	**super-**	
21.	**trans-, tra-**	

EXAMPLES

absent abrupt aberration abject

GREEK:

	PREFIX	MEANING
22.	a-, an-	
23.	anti-, ant-	
24.	apo-, ap-	
25.	cata-	
26.	dia-, di-	
27.	ec-	
28.	epi-, ep-	
29.	eu-	
30.	hetero-	
31.	homo-	
32.	hyper-	
33.	hypo-, hyp-	
34.	meta-, met-	
35.	micro-	
36.	orth-	
37.	para-, par-	
38.	peri-	
39.	syn-	
40.	tele-	

EXAMPLES

ANGLO-SAXON:

	Prefix	Meaning
41.	a-	
42.	be-	
43.	for-	
44.	fore-	
45.	n-	
46.	out-	
47.	over-	
48.	un-	
49.	under-	
50.	with-	

EXAMPLES

Latin Prefixes

Write a root-definition for each of the following words:

FER: *to carry, to bear*

interfere	*between — to carry*
transfer	
circumference	
infer	
suffer	
offer	
afferent	
efferent	
defer	
refer	
confer	
prefer	
proffer	

MIT, MISS: *to send*

intermittent	
intermission	
transmit	
transmission	
submit	
submission	
admit	
emit	

demise   _____

remit   _____

committee   _____

premise   _____

promise   _____

In each space write the words formed from the prefix-root combinations.

	DUC *to lead*	FER *to bear*	JECT *to throw*	SCRIB SCRIPT *to write*	PON POS *to put*
PRO- *forward*					
DE- *down* *away*					
RE- *back* *again*			reject rejected rejection		
IN-, IM- *in* *into*					
CON-, COM- *together* *with*					

Number Roots

Meaning	Root(s)
half	*hemi, demi, semi, med*
one	
two	
three	
four	
five	
six	
seven	
eight	
nine	
ten	
plus ten	
times ten	
hundred	
thousand	
ten thousand	
million	
first	
both	
equal	
few	
many	
all	

Examples

hemisphere   demitasse   semi-colon   medium

Suffixes

Suffix	Meaning
1. **-able**	*able to (be)*
2. **-ac, -iac**	
3. **-acious**	
4. **-acy, -cy**	
5. **-age**	
6. **-al**	
7. **-ance**	
8. **-ancy**	
9. **-ary, -arium**	
10. **-dom**	
11. **-ee**	
12. **-eer**	
13. **-en (v.)**	
14. **-ence**	
15. **-ency**	
16. **-er, -yer**	
17. **-ery**	
18. **-escent**	
19. **-esis**	
20. **-eur**	
21. **-ferous**	
22. **-fold**	
23. **-ful**	
24. **-fy**	
25. **-hood**	

EXAMPLES

adaptable   reliable   avoidable

	SUFFIX	MEANING
26.	-ic	
27.	-ical	
28.	-ier	
29.	-ine	
30.	-ion, -tion	
31.	-ish	
32.	-ism	
33.	-ist	
34.	-ium	
35.	-ive (adj.)	
36.	-ize, -ise	
37.	-less	
38.	-ly (adj.)	
39.	-ly (adv.)	
40.	-ness	
41.	-oid, -oda, -ode	
42.	-or	
43.	-ory, -orium	
44.	-ose	
45.	-ous	
46.	-ship	
47.	-some	
48.	-ulent	
49.	-ward	
50.	-wise	

EXAMPLES

Diminutives

Some diminutive suffixes:

-cle	-et	-kin	-ock	-y
-cule	-ette	-let	-ula	
-el	-ie	-ling	-ule	

Fill each of the blanks below with a word which uses a diminutive suffix.

1.	little book	B ___ o o k l e ___	T
2.	little James	J _____	Y
3.	little part	P _____	E
4.	little sphere	S _____	E
5.	little cigar	C _____	T
6.	little verse	V _____	E
7.	little relative	S _____	G
8.	little Paul	P _____	E
9.	little skin	C _____	E
10.	little prince	P _____	G
11.	little key	C _____	E
12.	little tablecloth	N _____	N
13.	little pig	P _____	T
14.	little body	C _____	E
15.	little pearl	M _____	E
16.	little man	M _____	N
17.	little closed place	C _____	T
18.	little bull	B _____	K
19.	little heap	M _____	E
20.	little precious one	D _____	G
21.	little joint	A _____	E
22.	little mouse	M _____	E

23.	little goose	G	_____	G
24.	little song	C	_____	E
25.	little hill	H	_____	K
26.	little box	C	_____	E
27.	son of little Will	W	_____	N
28.	little animal of one year	Y	_____	G
29.	little root	R	_____	E
30.	little lame one	C	_____	E
31.	little brain	C	_____	M
32.	little form	F	_____	A
33.	little finger-length fish	F	_____	G
34.	little something new	N	_____	L
35.	little stomach	G	_____	A
36.	little tree from a seed	S	_____	G
37.	little tree	S	_____	G
38.	little cell	C	_____	E
39.	little bud	B	_____	A
40.	little statue	S	_____	E
41.	little feathered one	F	_____	G
42.	little knot	N	_____	E
43.	little abandoned infant	F	_____	G
44.	little animal	A	_____	E
45.	little duck	D	_____	G
46.	little hanging thing	P	_____	M
47.	little (St.) Peter	P	_____	L
48.	little cat	K	_____	Y
49.	little-body device	C	_____	T
50.	son of little Tom	T	_____	N

Medical Roots

	Root	Meaning
1.	**aden**	*gland*
2.	**alg**	
3.	**angi**	
4.	**anter-**	
5.	**arthr, art**	
6.	**brady-**	
7.	**bronch**	
8.	**burs**	
9.	**card**	
10.	**cephal**	
11.	**chir, cheir**	
12.	**chol**	
13.	**chondr**	
14.	**cocc**	
15.	**crani**	
16.	**cyst**	
17.	**derm**	
18.	**ecto-**	
19.	**endo-**	
20.	**enter**	
21.	**gangli**	
22.	**gastr**	
23.	**hem, haem, em**	
24.	**hepat**	
25.	**hyster**	

EXAMPLES

adenoids   adenalgia   myxadenitis

	ROOT	MEANING
26.	-ia	
27.	-itis	
28.	mast	
29.	my	
30.	myel	
31.	nephr	
32.	neur	
33.	-oma	
34.	ophthalm	
35.	-osis, -sis	
36.	oste	
37.	ot	
38.	path	
39.	phleb	
40.	pneumon, pneum, pne	
41.	poster-	
42.	proct	
43.	psych	
44.	ren	
45.	rhin	
46.	-rrhea	
47.	stom	
48.	tach	
49.	tom, tme	
50.	trache	

EXAMPLES

Biological Roots

	Root	Meaning
1.	**amoeb**	*change, amoeba*
2.	**annel, annul**	
3.	**anth**	
4.	**auto-**	
5.	**bio**	
6.	**blast**	
7.	**bucc**	
8.	**capill**	
9.	**cav**	
10.	**cervic**	
11.	**chias**	
12.	**chord**	
13.	**chyl**	
14.	**chym**	
15.	**cili**	
16.	**clas**	
17.	**coel, cel**	
18.	**cyt**	
19.	**dur**	
20.	**eco-, oec**	
21.	**ento-**	
22.	**foramin**	
23.	**gen**	
24.	**gym**	
25.	**hist**	

EXAMPLES

amoebic   amoebiform   amoebotaenia

	Root	Meaning
26.	**lamin, lamell**	
27.	**lemm**	
28.	**macro-**	
29.	**meso-**	
30.	**nemat**	
31.	**ov**	
32.	**palp**	
33.	**phag**	
34.	**phyt**	
35.	**plas**	
36.	**pulm, pulmon**	
37.	**ram**	
38.	**sarc**	
39.	**scler**	
40.	**sinus, sinu**	
41.	**squam**	
42.	**thec**	
43.	**trich, thrix**	
44.	**vag**	
45.	**vagin**	
46.	**vesic**	
47.	**vita**	
48.	**vitell**	
49.	**zo**	
50.	**zyg, zeug**	

EXAMPLES

Animals in Words

	WORD	MEANING AND REASON
1.	**porcupine**	spiny pig—from appearance
2.	**canary**	
3.	**easel**	
4.	**dandelion**	
5.	**impecunious**	
6.	**halibut**	
7.	**Capri**	
8.	**cancer**	
9.	**chameleon**	
10.	**muscle**	
11.	**alligator**	
12.	**fellow**	
13.	**Alcatraz**	
14.	**bugle**	
15.	**Beverley**	
16.	**pedigree**	
17.	**chevron**	
18.	**polecat**	
19.	**formic acid**	
20.	**Turin**	
21.	**cab**	
22.	**cynosure**	
23.	**marshal**	
24.	**Arctic**	
25.	**cynic**	

	Word	Meaning and Reason
26.	chivalry	
27.	porcelain	
28.	hippopotamus	
29.	presbytery	
30.	peculiar	
31.	bellwether	
32.	Bernard	
33.	buffalo	
34.	porpoise	
35.	kennel	
36.	priest	
37.	aviator	
38.	cavalcade	

Animal Adjectives

	Word	Root	Animal
39.	canine	can	dog
40.	porcine		
41.	leonine		
42.	lupine		
43.	asinine		
44.	feline		
45.	bovine		
46.	aquiline		
47.	serpentine		
48.	piscine		
49.	vulpine		
50.	equine		

Colors in Words

	WORD	ROOT	COLOR
1.	chlorine	*chlor*	green
2.	melancholy		
3.	Argentina		
4.	iodine		
5.	chrysanthemum		
6.	rubric		
7.	albino		
8.	denigrate		
9.	leucocyte		
10.	chlorophyll		
11.	praseodymium		
12.	cirrhosis		
13.	fulvous		
14.	Ethiopia		
15.	iris		
16.	panchromatic		
17.	aureole		
18.	atrocious		
19.	bleachers		
20.	viridescent		
21.	Chrysostom		
22.	rhododendron		
23.	Maurice		
24.	albumen		
25.	rubella		

	WORD	ROOT	COLOR
26.	cyanosis		
27.	polio		
28.	argentiferous		
29.	Colorado		
30.	ruby		
31.	phoenix		
32.	flavid		
33.	caesium		
34.	chrysalis		
35.	Melanesia		
36.	platinum		
37.	leukemia		
38.	glaucoma		
39.	oriole		
40.	chromosome		
41.	Rhode Island		
42.	xanthoderma		
43.	cyanide		
44.	riboflavin		
45.	candidate		
46.	Blanche		
47.	appalling		
48.	edelweiss		
49.	Rufus		
50.	album		

People in Words

	WORD	NAME
1.	saxophone	*Antoine J. (Adolphe) Sax*
2.	maudlin	
3.	sadist	
4.	tawdry	
5.	pander	
6.	philippic	
7.	chauvinism	
8.	epicurean	
9.	quixotic	
10.	amazon	
11.	boycott	
12.	macadam	
13.	czar	
14.	solon	
15.	pants	
16.	martial	
17.	silhouette	
18.	derrick	
19.	volt	
20.	nicotine	
21.	dunce	
22.	crisscross	
23.	atlas	
24.	ammonia	
25.	camellia	

REASON

invented the instrument

	WORD	NAME
26.	panic	
27.	guillotine	
28.	lynch	
29.	mentor	
30.	cereal	
31.	America	
32.	tantalize	
33.	volcano	
34.	derby	
35.	guppy	
36.	sandwich	
37.	venereal	
38.	aphrodisiac	
39.	martinet	
40.	pasteurize	
41.	titanic	
42.	cardigan	
43.	morphine	
44.	masochist	
45.	maverick	
46.	groggy	
47.	brag	
48.	Bolivia	
49.	guy	
50.	mausoleum	

REASON

Places in Words

	WORD	PLACE
1.	**millinery**	*Milan, Italy*
2.	**bedlam**	
3.	**stoic**	
4.	**stygian**	
5.	**meander**	
6.	**labyrinth**	
7.	**pandemonium**	
8.	**maelstrom**	
9.	**laconic**	
10.	**olympian**	
11.	**academy**	
12.	**bourbon**	
13.	**cologne**	
14.	**frankfurter**	
15.	**artesian**	
16.	**cravat**	
17.	**wiener**	
18.	**denim**	
19.	**hamburger**	
20.	**peach**	
21.	**attic**	
22.	**tangerine**	
23.	**bayonet**	
24.	**currant**	
25.	**cantaloupe**	

REASON

center for women's finery in 16th Century

	WORD	PLACE
26.	solecism	
27.	copper	
28.	cashmere	
29.	calico	
30.	tuxedo	
31.	turquoise	
32.	sherry	
33.	port (wine)	
34.	gypsy	
35.	worsted	
36.	canary	
37.	limousine	
38.	damask	
39.	walnut	
40.	dollar	
41.	arras	
42.	vaudeville	
43.	bungalow	
44.	roquefort	
45.	canter	
46.	burgundy	
47.	indigo	
48.	magnet	
49.	sybaritic	
50.	spaniel	

REASON

Words from Latin—I

	WORD	ROOT-DEFINITION
1.	**contradict**	*against—to speak*
2.	**inspector**	
3.	**president**	
4.	**centigrade**	
5.	**refuge**	
6.	**dentifrice**	
7.	**loquacious**	
8.	**incredible**	
9.	**prelude**	
10.	**annihilate**	
11.	**magnify**	
12.	**progress**	
13.	**incisor**	
14.	**translate**	
15.	**decadent**	
16.	**independent**	
17.	**distort**	
18.	**omnivorous**	
19.	**contemporary**	
20.	**exit**	
21.	**innate**	
22.	**unison**	
23.	**aquamarine**	
24.	**decapitate**	
25.	**concourse**	

OTHER EXAMPLES

contrary   contrast   predict   dictionary

	WORD	ROOT-DEFINITION
26.	**subscribe**	
27.	**intersection**	
28.	**confide**	
29.	**revolution**	
30.	**anniversary**	
31.	**infinite**	
32.	**repulsive**	
33.	**immortal**	
34.	**attract**	
35.	**resist**	
36.	**nominate**	
37.	**conspiracy**	
38.	**corpulent**	
39.	**vivacious**	
40.	**concord**	
41.	**audition**	
42.	**verbose**	
43.	**paternity**	
44.	**interference**	
45.	**complex**	
46.	**proponent**	
47.	**consequent**	
48.	**missile**	
49.	**somnambulist**	
50.	**exclusive**	

OTHER EXAMPLES

Words from Latin–II

ROOT-DEFINITION	WORD
1. **out—to push**	*expel*
2. **after—to place**	
3. **gnaw—ing**	
4. **away—to scrape**	
5. **against—to build**	
6. **clear—to make**	
7. **back—into—bag**	
8. **not—injure—ing**	
9. **drag—that which**	
10. **three—teeth**	
11. **sacred—to make**	
12. **down—to laugh**	
13. **before—run—one who**	
14. **back—to bend**	
15. **not—strong—place where**	
16. **middle—age—related to**	
17. **out—root—to do**	
18. **together—seek—one who**	
19. **rule—ing**	
20. **all—know—ing**	
21. **not—please—able**	
22. **back—to bite**	
23. **apart—flock—to make**	
24. **twist—having the quality of**	
25. **pledge—one who**	

OTHER EXAMPLES

extricate   exodus   repellent   propeller

	ROOT-DEFINITION	WORD
26.	away—to advise	
27.	touch—ing	
28.	together—stars—state	
29.	to hold—having quality of	
30.	not—fit	
31.	one—shape	
32.	road—to lead	
33.	voice—bearing	
34.	together—run—ing	
35.	not—conquer—able	
36.	thoroughly—strong—becoming	
37.	forward—to thrust	
38.	in—to flow—act	
39.	witness—to make	
40.	through—breathe	
41.	sun—place where	
42.	without—care	
43.	not—out—to pray—able	
44.	rise—ing	
45.	many—side—related to	
46.	away—wash—act	
47.	bear—able—to make	
48.	not—together—stick—ing	
49.	out of—ground	
50.	toward—heavy—to make	

OTHER EXAMPLES

Words from Greek–I

	WORD	ROOT-DEFINITION
1.	**atom**	*not—cut*
2.	**cosmopolitan**	
3.	**pentagon**	
4.	**pantomime**	
5.	**schizophrenia**	
6.	**philanthropist**	
7.	**anonymous**	
8.	**telegram**	
9.	**tripod**	
10.	**chromosome**	
11.	**autonomy**	
12.	**odometer**	
13.	**monolithic**	
14.	**acrophobia**	
15.	**eucalyptus**	
16.	**megaphone**	
17.	**encephalitis**	
18.	**taxidermist**	
19.	**cardiac**	
20.	**amphibious**	
21.	**Cyclops**	
22.	**psychosomatic**	
23.	**photograph**	
24.	**atheist**	
25.	**sympathy**	

OTHER EXAMPLES

atypical   amoral   dichotomy   anatomy

	WORD	ROOT-DEFINITION
26.	chiropractor	
27.	technical	
28.	anemia	
29.	misanthropic	
30.	euthanasia	
31.	hippopotamus	
32.	pediatrician	
33.	bibliophile	
34.	microscope	
35.	autobiography	
36.	astronomy	
37.	geriatrics	
38.	diagnosis	
39.	amorphous	
40.	bigamist	
41.	geophysical	
42.	isotherm	
43.	neuritis	
44.	democrat	
45.	antipyretic	
46.	epitaph	
47.	geography	
48.	misogynist	
49.	orthodontia	
50.	trigonometry	

OTHER EXAMPLES

Words from Greek–II

	ROOT-DEFINITION	WORD
1.	solid—sound—related to	*stereophonic*
2.	copy—to write	
3.	heat—to measure	
4.	against—struggle—one who	
5.	down—to turn	
6.	black—bile—state	
7.	three—circle	
8.	home—order—related to	
9.	good—word—act	
10.	through—to flow	
11.	many—marriage—state	
12.	terrible—lizard	
13.	small—universe	
14.	mind—heal—one who	
15.	first—model	
16.	without—feeling—condition	
17.	time—measure	
18.	whole—to burn	
19.	man—study of	
20.	one—to rule	
21.	badly—nourished—state	
22.	joint—inflammation	
23.	up—cut—state	
24.	white—blood—condition	
25.	sun—element	

OTHER EXAMPLES

stereotype   cholesterol   phonetic   phonograph

	ROOT-DEFINITION	WORD
26.	around—measure	
27.	birth—act	
28.	together—name	
29.	under—skin	
30.	love—wisdom—one who	
31.	small—to look	
32.	sign—to carry	
33.	not—remember—condition	
34.	all—view	
35.	straight—child—one who	
36.	green—leaf	
37.	without—feeling—state	
38.	colored—body	
39.	hidden—to write	
40.	to digest—related to	
41.	without—rule—state	
42.	to love—tree	
43.	good—death—condition	
44.	blood—to flow	
45.	light—measure	
46.	beyond—to carry	
47.	new—plant	
48.	together—arrangement	
49.	around—to look	
50.	wise—stupid	

OTHER EXAMPLES

Words from One Root

GEN: *cause, birth, kind, race*

1. to cause
   GENerate

2. a cause of electricity
   G E N _ _ _ _ _ r

3. to cause anew
   _ _ G E N _ _ a _ _

4. a chemical cause of water
   _ y _ _ _ G E N

5. a chemical cause of niter
   _ _ _ _ o G E N

6. (a condition) caused by the mind (adj.)
   p _ _ _ _ _ G E N _ _

7. causing a good photograph
   _ _ _ _ _ G E N _ c

8. birth
   G E N _ _ i _

9. tending to give birth
   G E N _ _ _ _ _ v _

10. to beget
    _ _ G E N d _ _

11. one who begets
    p _ _ G E N _ _ _ _

12. one set of births
    G E N _ _ _ _ i _ _

13. relating to heredity

    G E N _ t _ _

14. the study of heredity

    G E N _ _ _ _ s

15. that which transmits hereditary traits

    G E N _

16. a study of births (family tree)

    G E N _ a _ _ _ _

17. offspring

    _ r _ G E N _

18. mating superior human beings

    e _ G E N _ _ _

19. pertaining to reproduction

    G E N _ _ _ l

20. the organs of reproduction

    G E N _ t _ _ _

21. existing from birth

    _ o _ G E N _ _ _ _

22. the origin of man

    a _ _ _ _ _ _ _ G E N _ _ _ _

23. native born (not imported)

    _ _ d _ G E N _ _ _

24. leaving the estate to the first-born male

    _ _ _ _ _ G E N _ _ u _ _

25. well-born (proper name)

    _ _ G E N e

26. refined (well-born)

    G E N _ _ e _

27. refinement

    G E N _ _ _ _ _ y

28. one who is born brilliant

    G E N i _ _

29. having inborn talent; clever

    i _ G E N _ _ _ _

30. of good (family) stock; magnanimous

    G E N _ r _ _ _

31. the well-born class (now usually humorous)

    G E N t _ _

32. gifted at birth; happy

    G E N _ a _

33. of a kind to be happy with others

    _ o _ G E N _ _ _

34. a man who is "well-born" and refined

    G E N _ _ _ m _ _

35. freeborn, frank, simple, gullible

    _ _ G E N u _ _ _

36. a simple, naive girl

    i _ G E N _ _

37. to fall away from the (good) kind

    _ _ G E N _ _ _ _ e

38. a major class or kind

    G E N u _

39. a sexual class or kind

    G E N _ _ r

40. an artistic class or kind

    G E N r _

41. pertaining to a class or kind

    G E N _ _ i _

42. pertaining to all of a class or kind

    G E N _ _ _ l

43. of the true kind; authentic

    G E N _ i _ _

44. of the same kind throughout

    h _ _ _ G E N _ _ _ _

45. made to be of the same kind throughout

    _ _ _ _ G E N _ z _ _

46. composed of different kinds

    _ _ t _ _ _ G E N _ _ _ _

47. a group of individuals of the same kind (biol.)

    GE N _ _ _ p _

48. a member of the non-Jewish race

    G E N _ _ _ e

49. mixture of races

    m _ _ _ _ G E N _ _ _ _ _

50. killing of a race

    G E N _ _ _ d _

Word-Pairs

1. **together—to suffer—state**

```
          s
          y
          m
c o m P a s s i o n
          a
          t
          h
          y
```

2. **under—to put—act**

```
    s
    -
    -
    -
h - - O - - - - - s
    -
    -
    -
    -
    n
```

3. **around—to look**

```
        c
        -
        -
        -
        -
p - - - S - - - e
        -
        -
        -
        t
```

4. **together—living**

```
    s
    -
    -
    -
c - - - I - - - l
    -
    -
    -
    c
```

326

5. **together—time**

```
          s
      c - N - - - - - - - - - -
          -
          -
          -
          -
          -
          -
          -
          -
          -
```

```
          c
          -
          -
          -
          -
      p - - - - - E - -
          -
          -
          -
          -
          -
```

6. **around—to carry**

7. **right-angled**

```
          o
          -
          -
          -
      r - - - - - G - - - -
          -
          -
          -
          -
```

```
          m
          -
          -
          -
      m - - I - - - -
          -
          -
          -
```

8. **many-fold**

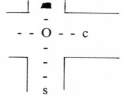

9. **love—having the quality of**

10. **over—to see—one who**

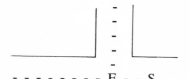

11. **below—skin—related to**

12. **many-tongued**

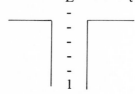

13. **bear—related to**

14. **together—to run**

15. **through—to turn—act**

16. **into—body**

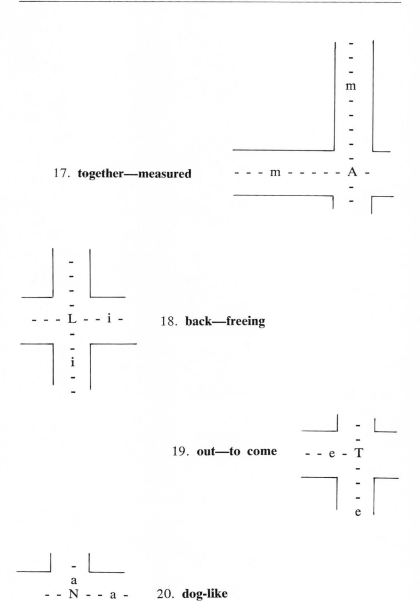

17. **together—measured**

18. **back—freeing**

19. **out—to come**

20. **dog-like**

Word-Chain

Find the missing links.

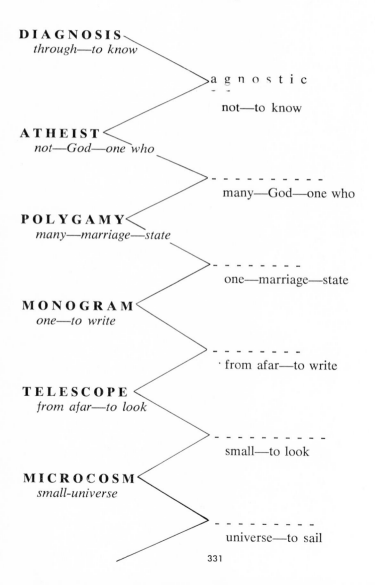

DIAGNOSIS
through—to know

a g n o s t i c

not—to know

ATHEIST
not—God—one who

- - - - - - - - -
many—God—one who

POLYGAMY
many—marriage—state

- - - - - - -
one—marriage—state

MONOGRAM
one—to write

- - - - - - - -
from afar—to write

TELESCOPE
from afar—to look

- - - - - - - - -
small—to look

MICROCOSM
small-universe

- - - - - - - -
universe—to sail

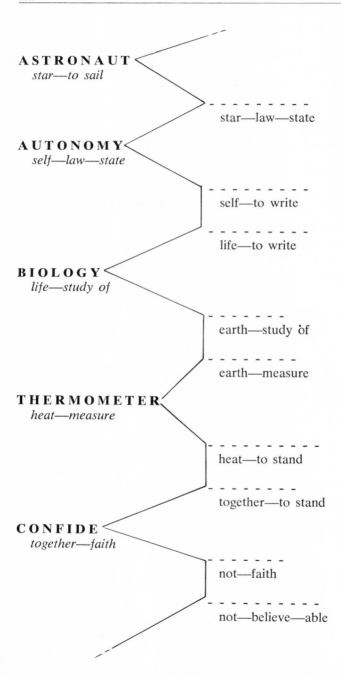

ASTRONAUT
star—to sail

- - - - - - - - -
star—law—state

AUTONOMY
self—law—state

- - - - - - - - -
self—to write

- - - - - - - - -
life—to write

BIOLOGY
life—study of

- - - - - - -
earth—study of

- - - - - - -
earth—measure

THERMOMETER
heat—measure

- - - - - - - - -
heat—to stand

- - - - - - - - -
together—to stand

CONFIDE
together—faith

- - - - - -
not—faith

- - - - - - - - -
not—believe—able

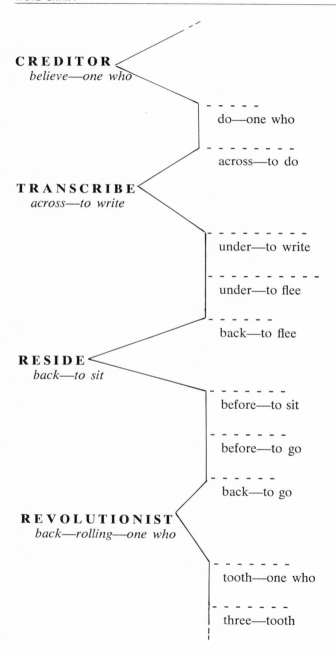

CREDITOR
believe—one who

- - - - -
do—one who

- - - - - - -
across—to do

TRANSCRIBE
across—to write

- - - - - - - -
under—to write

- - - - - - - - - -
under—to flee

- - - - - -
back—to flee

RESIDE
back—to sit

- - - - - - -
before—to sit

- - - - - - -
before—to go

- - - - - -
back—to go

REVOLUTIONIST
back—rolling—one who

- - - - - -
tooth—one who

- - - - - -
three—tooth

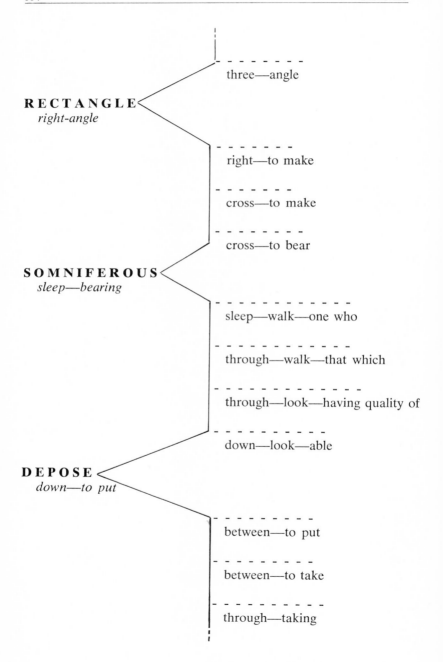

RECTANGLE
right-angle

three—angle

right—to make

cross—to make

cross—to bear

SOMNIFEROUS
sleep—bearing

sleep—walk—one who

through—walk—that which

through—look—having quality of

down—look—able

DEPOSE
down—to put

between—to put

between—to take

through—taking

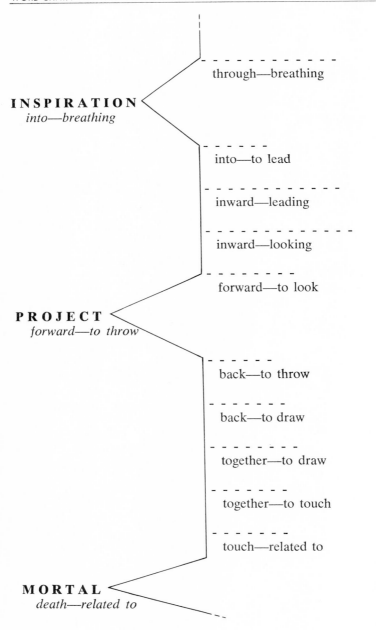

INSPIRATION
into—breathing

through—breathing

into—to lead

inward—leading

inward—looking

forward—to look

PROJECT
forward—to throw

back—to throw

back—to draw

together—to draw

together—to touch

touch—related to

MORTAL
death—related to

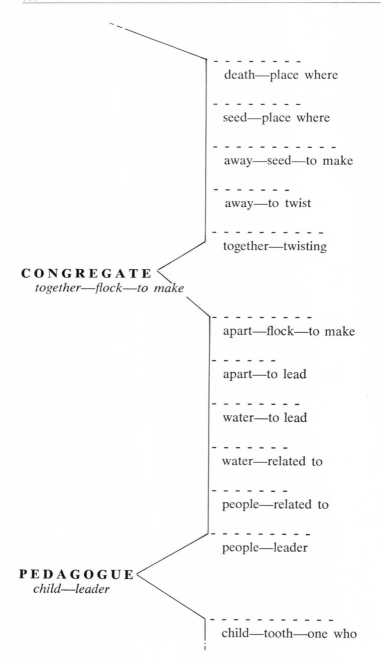

- - - - - - - -
death—place where

- - - - - - - -
seed—place where

- - - - - - - - - -
away—seed—to make

- - - - - - -
away—to twist

- - - - - - - - -
together—twisting

CONGREGATE
together—flock—to make

- - - - - - - -
apart—flock—to make

- - - - - -
apart—to lead

- - - - - - - -
water—to lead

- - - - - - -
water—related to

- - - - - - -
people—related to

- - - - - - - -
people—leader

PEDAGOGUE
child—leader

- - - - - - - - - -
child—tooth—one who

straight—tooth—one who

straight—write—act

shake—write—act

shake—measure

head—measure—act

ENCEPHALITIS
in—head—inflammation

nose—inflammation

nose—to look

ear—to look

ear—study of

fungus—study of

earth—fungus

middle—earth—related to

INTERMEDIARY
between—middle—one who

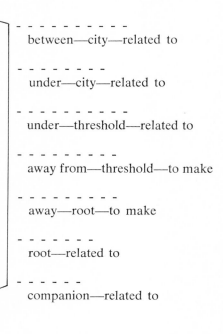

between—city—related to

under—city—related to

under—threshold—related to

away from—threshold—to make

away—root—to make

root—related to

companion—related to

SOCIETY
companion—state

Bibliography

STANDARD AND ETYMOLOGICAL DICTIONARIES

The American College Dictionary. New York: Random House, 1962. 1444 pp.

Collocott, T. C. (ed.), *Chambers' English Dictionary.* Totowa, N.J.: Littlefield, Adams & Co. (SOS 166), 1965. 380 pp., paper.

Gove, Philip B. (ed.), *Webster's Third New International Dictionary.* Springfield, Mass.: 1963. 2662 pp.

MacDonald, A. M. (ed.), *Chambers' Etymological English Dictionary.* Totowa, N.J.: Littlefield, Adams & Co. (SOS 153), 1964. 784 pp., paper.

Matthews, Mitford, *Dictionary of Americanisms,* one volume edition. Chicago: University of Chicago Press, 1951. 1946 pp.

Murray, James A. H. (ed.), *Oxford English Dictionary.* 13 vols. Oxford: Clarendon Press, 1961.

Onions, C. T. (ed.), *The Oxford Universal Dictionary.* Oxford: Clarendon Press, 1955. 2515 pp.

Partridge, Eric, *Origins, a Short Etymological Dictionary of Modern English.* New York: The Macmillan Company, 1961. 972 pp.

Shipley, Joseph T., *Dictionary of Word Origins.* Totowa, N.J.: Littlefield, Adams & Co. (SOS 121), 1964. 430 pp., paper.

Skeat, Walter W., *A Concise Etymological Dictionary of the English Language.* New York: Capricorn Books (Cap Giant 235), 1963. 656 pp.

Standard College Dictionary. New York: Harcourt, Brace & World, 1963. 1606 pp.

Webster's New World Dictionary of the American Language. New York: The World Publishing Company, 1951. 1724 pp.

Webster's Seventh New Collegiate Dictionary. Springfield, Mass.: G. & C. Merriam Co., 1963. 1220 pp.

MEDICAL AND BIOLOGICAL TERMINOLOGY

Abercrombie, M., C. J. Hickman and M. L. Johnson, *A Dictionary of Biology.* Baltimore: Penguin Books (R 3), 1951. 254 pp., paper.

Agard, Walter R., and Herbert M. Howe, *Medical Greek and Latin at a Glance.* New York: Harper & Brothers (Hoeber-Harper Books), 1960. 96 pp.

Dorland's Illustrated Medical Dictionary. Philadelphia: W. B. Saunders Co., 1957. 1598 pp.

Jaeger, Edmund C., *A Source-Book of Biological Names and Terms,* 3rd edition. Springfield, Ill.: Charles C. Thomas, 1955. 323 pp.

Medical Etymology, teaching copy, reprinted from *Stedman's Medical Dictionary,* 20th edition. Baltimore: The Williams & Wilkins Co., 1961. 31 pp., paper.

Pepper, O. H. Perry, *Medical Etymology.* Philadelphia: W. B. Saunders Co., 1959. 263 pp.

Schifferes, Justus J., *Schifferes' Family Medical Encyclopedia.* New York: Permabooks (M 5013), 1959. 619 pp., paper.

Skinner, Henry Alan, *The Origin of Medical Terms,* 2nd edition. Baltimore: The Williams & Wilkins Co., 1961. 438 pp.

Stedman's Medical Dictionary, 20th edition. Baltimore: The Williams & Wilkins Co., 1961. 1680 pp.

Swartz, Harry, *Layman's Medical Dictionary.* New York: Frederick Ungar Publishing Co., 1955. 306 pp., paper.

Yancy, Patrick H., S. J., *Origins from Mythology of Biological Names and Terms,* 2nd edition. Mobile, Ala.: Spring Hill College Press, 1961. 47 pp., paper.

SCIENTIFIC TERMINOLOGY

English, Horace B., and Ava C. English, *A Comprehensive Dictionary of Psychological and Phychoanalytical Terms.* New York: Longmans, Green & Co., 1959. 595 pp.

Flood, W. E., *Dictionary of Chemical Names.* Totowa, N.J.: Littlefield, Adams & Co. (SOS 147), 1963. 238 pp., paper.

Gaynor, Frank, *Concise Dictionary of Science.* Totowa, N.J.: Littlefield, Adams & Co. (SOS 106), 1964. 546 pp., paper.

Gundlach, Bernard H., *The Laidlaw Glossary of Arithmetical-Mathematical Terms.* Palo Alto, Calif.: Laidlaw Brothers, Publishers, 1961. 120 pp., paper.

Handel, S., *A Dictionary of Electronics.* Baltimore: Penguin Books, Inc. (R 19), 1962. 384 pp., paper.

Harriman, P. L., *Dictionary of Psychology.* New York: The Wisdom Library (Philosophical Library), 1947. 364 pp., paper.

Hough, John N., *Scientific Terminology.* New York: Rinehart & Co., 1954. 231 pp.

National Radio Institute Teaching Staff, *Radio-Television Electronics Dictionary*. New York: John F. Rider Publisher, 1962. 190 pp., paper.

Spitz, Armand & Frank Gaynor, *Dictionary of Astronomy and Astronautics*. Totowa, N.J.: Littlefield, Adams & Co. (SOS 107), 1960. 439 pp., paper.

Tweney, C. F., & L. E. C. Hughes (eds.), *Chamber's Technical Dictionary*. New York: The Macmillan Company, 1961. 1028 pp.

Uvarov, E. B., and D. R. Chapman, *A Dictionary of Science*. Baltimore: Penguin Books (R 1), 1951. 240 pp., paper.

FOREIGN LANGUAGE DICTIONARIES

Andrews, E. A. (ed.), *Harper's Latin Dictionary*. New York: Harper & Brothers, 1880. 2019 pp.

Betteridge, Harold T. (ed.), *The New Cassell's German Dictionary*. New York: Funk & Wagnalls Co., 1962. 630 & 619 pp.

The Classic Greek Dictionary. Chicago: Follett Publishing Co., 1962. 835 & 262 pp.

Deak, Etienne & Simone, *A Dictionary of Colorful French Slanguage and Colloquialisms*. New York: E. P. Dutton & Co. (Dutton Paperback D 87), 1961. 210 pp., paper.

Gerrard, A. Bryson, & Jose de Heras Heras, *Cassell's Beyond the Dictionary in Spanish*. New York: Funk & Wagnalls Company, Inc., 1964. 160 pp.

Girard, Denis (ed.), *The New Cassell's French Dictionary*. New York: Funk & Wagnalls Co., Inc., 1962. 762 & 655 pp.

Glendening, P. J. T., *Cassell's Beyond the Dictionary in Italian*. New York: Funk & Wagnalls Co., Inc., 1964. 159 pp.

Klatt, E., & G. Golze, *Langenscheidt's German-English English-German Dictionary*. New York: Pocket Books, Inc. (GC 7), 1954. 526 pp., paper.

Larousse's French-English English-French Dictionary. New York: Pocket Books, Inc. (GC 24), 1960. 256 & 260 pp., paper.

Liddell, Henry George, & Robert Scott, *A Greek-English Lexicon*. New York: Harper & Brothers, 1868. 1705 pp.

Monadori's Pocket Italian-English English-Italian Dictionary. New York: Pocket Books, Inc. (GC 47), 1960. 271 & 305 pp., paper.

Peers, Edgar A., Jose V. Barragan, Francesco A. Vinzals, and Jorge A. Mora (eds.), *Cassell's Spanish Dictionary*. New York: Funk & Wagnalls Co., Inc., 1960. xvi & 1477 pp.

Rebora, Piero (ed.), *Cassell's Italian Dictionary*. New York: Funk
& Wagnalls Co., Inc., 1964. xxi & 1096 pp.
Simpson, D. P. (ed.), *Cassell's New Compact Latin-English
English-Latin Dictionary*. New York: Funk & Wagnalls Co.,
Inc., 1963. 379 pp.
————————— (ed.), *Cassell's New Latin Dictionary*. New York:
Funk & Wagnalls Co., Inc., 1959. xviii & 883 pp.
*The University of Chicago Spanish-English English-Spanish Dic-
tionary*. New York: Pocket Books, Inc. (C 122), 1960. 226
& 252 pp., paper.

SPECIALIZED DICTIONARIES

Abrams, M. H., *A Glossary of Literary Terms*. New York: Holt,
Rinehart & Winston, 1964. 105 pp., paper.
American Geological Institute, *Dictionary of Geological Terms*.
Garden City, New York: Doubleday & Co., Inc. (Dolphin
C 360), 1962. 545 pp., paper.
Andrews, Wayne (ed.), *Concise Dictionary of American History*.
New York: Charles Scribner's Sons, 1962. 1156 pp.
Barnet, Sylvan, Morton Berman, and William Burto, *A Dictionary
of Literary Terms*. Boston: Little, Brown & Co., 1960. 96
pp., paper.
Bierce, Ambrose, *The Devil's Dictionary*. New York: Dover Pub-
lications Inc., 1958. 145 pp., paper.
Burgess, F. H., *A Dictionary of Sailing*. Baltimore: Penguin Books,
Inc. (R 18), 1961. 237 pp., paper.
Cohen, J. M., and M. J. Cohen, *The Penguin Dictionary of Quota-
tions*. Baltimore: Penguin Books, Inc. (R 16), 1963. 664
pp., paper.
Colby, Frank O., *University Pronouncing Dictionary of Trouble-
some Words*. New York: Thomas Y. Crowell Co. (Apollo
A 94), 1964. 399 pp., paper.
Devlin, Joseph, *A Dictionary of Snyonyms and Antonyms*. New
York: Popular Library, Inc. (W 1107), 1961. 384 pp.,
paper.
Elliott, Florence, and Michael Summerskill, *A Dictionary of
Politics*. Baltimore: Penguin Books (R 10), 1964. 396 pp.,
paper.
Evans, Bergen, and Cornelia Evans, *A Dictionary of Contemporary
American Usage*. New York: Random House, 1957. 567 pp.
Ewen, David, *Encyclopedia of Concert Music*. New York: Hill &
Wang, 1959. 566 pp.
————————————, *Encyclopedia of the Opera*. New York: Hill &
Wang, 1963. 594 pp.

Fowler, H. W., *A Dictionary of Modern English Usage*. Oxford: Clarendon Press, 1961. 742 pp.

Freeman, John (ed.), *Brewer's Dictionary of Phrase and Fable*. New York: Harper & Row, 1963. 970 pp.

Goldin, Hyman E., et al., *Dictionary of American Underworld Lingo*. New York: The Citadel Press (C 113), 1962. 327 pp., paper.

Gregg, John R., et al., *Gregg Shorthand Dictionary*. New York: McGraw-Hill, 1963. 376 pp.

Hastings, James (ed.), *Dictionary of the Bible,* revised edition. New York: Charles Scribner's Sons, 1963. 1059 pp.

Hopkins, Joseph G. E. (ed.), *Concise Dictionary of American Biography*. New York: Charles Scribner's Sons, 1964. 1273 pp.

Jacobs, Arthur, *A New Dictionary of Music*. Baltimore: Penguin Books, Inc. (R 12), 1963. 416 pp., paper.

Johnson, Burges, *New Rhyming Dictionary and Poet's Handbook,* revised edition. New York: Harper & Row, Publishers, Inc., 1957. 464 pp.

Jordan, Joseph, *A Handbook for Terrible Spellers, the backwords dictionary*. New York: Innovation Press (331 Madison Ave.), 1964. 44 pp., paper.

Kirkwood, G. M., *A Short Guide to Classical Mythology*. New York: Holt, Rinehart and Winston, 1959. 109 pp., paper.

Kling, Samuel G., *The Legal Encyclopedia for Home and Business*. New York: Permabooks (M 5012), 1959. 565 pp., paper.

Levinson, Leonard Louis, *The Left Handed Dictionary*. New York: Collier Books (AS 495), 1963. 254 pp., paper.

Lewis, Norman, *Comprehensive Word Guide to the English Language*. Garden City, N.Y.: Doubleday & Co., Inc., 1958. 912 pp.

Mawson, C. O. Sylvester, *Dictionary of Foreign Terms*. New York: Bantam Books (NR 35), 1961. 335 pp., paper.

Mayberry, George, *A Concise Dictionary of Abbreviations*. New York: Tudor Publishing Co., 1961. 159 pp.

McAdam, E. L., Jr., and George Milne, *Johnson's Dictionary, a modern selection*. New York: Pantheon Books (Random House), 1963. 465 pp.

Moore, W. G., *A Dictionary of Geography*. Baltimore: Penguin Books (R 2), 1963. 196 pp., paper.

Murray, Peter, and Linda Murray, *A Dictionary of Art and Artists*. Baltimore: Penguin Books, Inc. (R 14), 1959. 355 pp., paper.

Nevins, Albert J., M. M. (ed.), *The Maryknoll Catholic Diction-*

ary. New York: Dimension Books (Grosset & Dunlap), 1965. 710 pp.

Newmark, Maxim, *Dictionary of Foreign Words.* Totowa, N.J.: Littlefield, Adams & Co. (SOS 142), 1962. 245 pp., paper.

The Oxford Dictionary of Quotations, 2nd edition. New York: Oxford University Press, 1955. 1003 pp.

Partridge, Eric, *A Dictionary of Cliches.* New York: E. P. Dutton & Co. (D 128), 1963. 259 pp., paper.

———————, *A Dictionary of Slang and Unconventional English.* New York: Macmillan.

———————, *Shakespeare's Bawdy.* New York: E. P. Dutton & Co. (D 55), 1960. 226 pp.

Prochnow, Herbert, *A Dictionary of Wit, Wisdom and Satire.* New York: Harper & Row, Publishers, Inc., 1962. 243 pp.

Roget's International Thesaurus, 3rd edition. New York: Thomas Y. Crowell Co., 1962. 1258 pp.

Schwartz, Robert J., *The Complete Dictionary of Abbreviations.* New York: Thomas Y. Crowell Co., 1959. 211 pp.

Seyffert, Oskar, *Dictionary of Classical Antiquities.* New York: Meridian Books, Inc. (ML 2) 1960. 716 pp., paper.

Shipley, Joseph T., *Dictionary of Early English.* Totowa, N.J.: Littlefield, Adams & Co. (SOS 150), 1963. 753 pp., paper.

Smith, Sir William, *Smaller Classical Dictionary.* New York: E. P. Dutton & Co. (D 12), 1958. 319 pp., paper.

Soule, Richard, *Soule's Dictionary of English Synonyms.* New York: Bantam Books (NR 9), 1961. 528 pp., paper.

Webster's Biographical Dictionary. Springfield, Mass.: G. & C. Merriam Co., 1962. 1698 pp.

Webster's Dictionary of Synonyms. Springfield, Mass.: G. & C. Merriam Co., 1951. 907 pp.

Webster's Geographical Dictionary. Springfield, Mass.: G. & C. Merriam Co., 1962. 1293 pp.

Wentworth, Harold, and Stuart Berg Flexner, *Dictionary of American Slang.* New York: Thomas Y. Crowell Co., 1960. 669 pp.

Zimmerman, John E., *Dictionary of Classical Mythology.* New York: Harper & Row, 1964. 256 pp.

BOOKS ABOUT PROPER NAMES

Ames, Winthrop, *What Shall we Name the Baby?* New York: Simon & Schuster, 1963. 187 pp., paper.

Foreign Versions of English Names. Washington, D.C.: U.S. Govt. Printing Office (M 131, 30c), 1962. Paper.

Gudde, Erwin G., *California Place Names*. Berkeley, California: University of California Press, 1962. 383 pp.

Patridge, Eric, *Name This Child, a dictionary of given or Christian names*. London: Hamish Hamilton, 1963. 126 pp.

Pei, Mario, and Eloise Lambert, *The Book of Place Names*. New York: Lothrop, Lee & Shepard Co., 1961. 178 pp.

Rule, Lareina, *Name Your Baby*. New York: Bantam Books (SR 40), 1963. 210 pp.

Sanchez, Nellie Van de Grift, *Spanish and Indian Place Names of California*. San Francisco: A. M. Robertson, 1922. 454 pp.

Smith, Elsdon C., *Dictionary of American Family Names*. New York: Harper & Brothers, 1956. 244 pp.

Stewart, George R., *Names on the Land*. Boston: Houghton-Miflin, 1958.

BOOKS ABOUT WORDS

Adams, J. Donald, *The Magic and Mystery of Words*. New York: Holt, Rinehart & Winston, 1963. 117 pp.

Brown, Ivor, *A Word in Your Ear,* and *Just Another Word*. New York: E. P. Dutton & Co., 1945. 136 & 128 pp.

Evans, Bergen, *Comfortable Words*. New York: Random House, 1962. 379 pp.

Funk, Charles Earle, *Heavens to Betsy! and other curious sayings*. New York: Harper & Row, 1955. 224 pp.

————————, *A Hog on Ice and other curious expressions*. New York: Harper & Row, 1948. 214 pp.

————————, and Charles Earle Funk, Jr., *Horsefeathers and other curious words*. New York: Harper & Row, 1958. 240 pp.

————————, *Thereby Hangs a Tale, stories of curious word origins*. New York: Harper & Row, 1950. 303 pp.

Funk, Wilfred, *Word Origins and Their Romantic Stories*. New York: Grosset & Dunlap, 1950. 432 pp.

Gardner, Martin (ed.), *Oddities and Curiosities of Words and Literature,* by C. C. Bombaugh. New York: Dover Publications, Inc. (T 759), 1961. 375 pp., paper.

Greenough, James B., and George Lyman Kittredge, *Words and Their Ways in English Speech*. New York: Macmillan Paperbacks (MP 65), 1961. 431 pp., paper.

Hixson, Jerome C., and I. Colodny, *Word Ways, a study of our living language*. New York: American Book Company, 1939. 338 pp.

Levitt, John, and Joan Levitt, *The Spell of Words*. New York: The Philosophical Library, 1959. 224 pp.

Lewis, C. S., *Studies in Words*. Cambridge: University Press, 1961. 240 pp.

Lewis, Norman, *New Power with Words*. New York: Thomas Y. Crowell, 1964. 326 pp.

——————, *Word Power Made Easy*. New York: Permabooks (M 4020), 1955. 457 pp., paper.

Mathews, Mitford M., *American Words*. New York: World Publishing Co., 1959. 246 pp.

Moore, John, *You English Words*. New York: J. B. Lippincott Co., 1962. 254 pp.

Morris, William, and Mary Morris, *Dictionary of Word and Phrase Origins*. New York: Harper & Row, 1962. 376 pp.

Nurnberg, Maxwell, and Morris Rosenblum, *How to Build a Better Vocabulary*. New York: Popular Library (SP 114), 1961. 382 pp., paper.

Partridge, Eric, *Adventuring Among Words*. New York: Oxford University Press, 1961. 72 pp.

Pei, Mario, *The Families of Words*. New York: Harper & Brothers, 1962. 288 pp.

Picturesque Word Origins. Springfield, Mass.: G. & C. Merriam Co., 1933. 134 pp.

Pyles, Thomas, *Words and Ways of American English*. New York: Random House, 1952. 310 pp., paper.

Radford, Edwin, *Unusual Words*. New York: Philosophical Library, 1946. 318 pp.

Wedeck, Harry E., *Short Dictionary of Classical Word Origins*. New York: Philosophical Library, 1957. 85 pp.

Weekley, Ernest, *The Romance of Words*. New York: Dover Publications, Inc., 1961. 175 pp., paper.

Wolverton, Robert E., *Classical Elements in English Words*. Totowa, N.J.: Littlefield, Adams & Co., 1965. 85 pp., paper.

BOOKS ABOUT LANGUAGE

Alexander, Henry, *The Story of Our Language*. Garden City, N.Y.: Dolphin Books (C 383), Doubleday & Co., 1962. 240 pp.

Bloomfield, Leonard, *Language*. New York: Holt, Rinehart and Winston, Inc., 1933.

Bloomfield, Morton W., and Leonard D. Newmark, *A Linguistic Introduction to the History of English*. New York: Alfred A. Knopf, Publisher, 1963. 416 pp.

Brook, G. L., *A History of the English Language*. New York:

W. W. Norton & Co., 1958. 224 pp., paper.

Chase, Stuart, *The Tyranny of Words*. New York: Harcourt, Brace & Co., 1938. 396 pp.

Cleator, P. E., *Lost Languages*. New York: New American Library (Mentor MT 427), 1959. 192 pp., paper.

Gleason, H. A., *An Introduction to Descriptive Linguistics*. New York: Holt, Rinehart & Winston, 1961. viii & 503 pp.

Hall, Robert A., *Linguistics and Your Language*. Garden City, N.Y.: Doubleday & Co. (Anchor Books A 201), 1960. 265 pp., paper.

Hogben, Lancelot, *The Mother Tongue*. New York: W. W. Norton, 1965. 294 pp.

Hughes, John P., *The Science of Language, an introduction to linguistics*. New York: Random House, 1962. 305 pp.

Jesperson, Otto, *Growth and Structure of the English Language*. Garden City, N.Y.: Doubleday Anchor Books (A 46), 1905. 274 pp., paper.

—————————, *Language, Its Nature, Development and Origin*. New York: W. W. Norton Co., 1964. 448 pp., paper.

Laird, Charlton, *The Miracle of Language*. New York: The World Publishing Co., 1953. 308 pp.

—————————, *Thinking about Language*. New York: Holt, Rinehart & Winston, 1964. 75 pp., paper.

Laird, Helene, and Charlton Laird, *The Tree of Language*. New York: The World Publishing Company, 1957. 235 pp.

Marckwardt, Albert H., *Introduction to the English Language*. New York: Oxford University Press, 1951. 347 pp.

Mencken, H. L., *The American Language,* one volume abridged edition of the 4th edition and two supplements. New York: Alfred A. Knopf, 1963. 777 & cxxiv pp.

Muller, Siegfried H., *The World's Living Languages*. New York: Frederick Ungar Publishing Company, 1964. 212 pp.

Potter, Simeon, *Modern Linguistics*. New York: W. W. Norton & Co., 1964. 192 pp., paper.

—————————, *Our Language*. Baltimore: Penguin Books (A 227), 1953. 202 pp., paper.

Pyles, Thomas, *The Origins and Development of The English Language*. New York: Harcourt, Brace & World, 1964. 388 pp.

New York: Harcourt, Brace & World, 1949 (and Harvest Books, 1955).

Tauber, Abraham, *George Bernard Shaw on Language*. New York: Philosophical Library, 1963. 205 pp.

Work-Pages

Root	Meaning

EXAMPLES

Root	Meaning

EXAMPLES

Root	Meaning

EXAMPLES

Root	Meaning

EXAMPLES

Root	Meaning

EXAMPLES

ROOT	MEANING

EXAMPLES

Root	Meaning

EXAMPLES

Root	Meaning

EXAMPLES

ROOT	MEANING

EXAMPLES

Root	Meaning

EXAMPLES

Root	Meaning

EXAMPLES

ROOT	MEANING

EXAMPLES

Root	Meaning

EXAMPLES